Sweet SAMPLES from Scripture

Pastor Walter Henry Cross

A Devotional for Sunday School Scholars

Sweet Samples from Scripture

A Devotional for Sunday School Scholars

by Pastor Walter Henry Cross

Copyright © 2020 Pastor Walter Henry Cross

All rights reserved. No part of this book may be reproduced or transmitted in any form or by any means, electronic or mechanical, including photocopying, recording or by any information storage and retrieval system without the written permission of the author or publisher, except for the inclusion of brief quotations in a review or article, when credit to the book, author, publisher, and order information are included in the review or article.

ISBN 978-0-9790251-6-7

Printed in the United States of America

Text and Cover Design by Debbie Patrick, www.debbiepatrick.com

Photo credits: istockphoto.com zepp1969 (cover) and istockphoto.com Nevov (chocolates)

Unless otherwise marked, all Scriptures are taken from the HOLY BIBLE, NEW LIVING TRANSLATION. (NLT): Scriptures taken from the HOLY BIBLE, NEW LIVING TRANSLATION, Copyright© 1996, 2004, 2007 by Tyndale House Foundation. Used by permission of Tyndale House Publishers, Inc., Carol Stream, Illinois 60188. All rights reserved. Used by permission.

Scriptures marked ESV are taken from the THE HOLY BIBLE, ENGLISH STANDARD. VERSION (ESV): Scriptures taken from THE HOLY BIBLE, ENGLISH STANDARD VERSION • Copyright© 2001 by Crossway, a publishing ministry of Good News Publishers. Used by permission.

Scriptures marked TLB are taken from the THE LIVING BIBLE (TLB): Scripture taken from THE LIVING BIBLE copyright© 1971. Used by permission of Tyndale House Publishers, Inc., Carol Stream, Illinois 60188. All rights reserved.

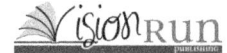

Vision Run Publishing
305 Portsmouth Rd.
Knoxville TN 37909
visionrun.com

*Dedicated to the glory
of God*

Acknowledgements

I'd like to extend special thanks to those who provided help, assistance and encouragement to make this book come into being.

First, Reverand Doctor Angela Hardy Cross, who shares my work, my life and my passion to serve God through loving his people. Next, Sister Dorothy Brady, Reverand Doctor Sharon Bowers, The Martin Chapel United Methodist Church family, The Lonsdale United Methodist Church family, and a special thanks to Pastor David Russell, serving Fellowship Church in Knoxville, and the world.

My gratitude to you all.

Pastor Walter "Old Rugged" Cross

Contents

Foreword 9

Year End and Birth of Christ 13

New Beginnings 39

Springtime: New Growth 81

Jonah 111

God with Us 129

God's Promises 191

Covenant Lessons 209

Faith and Joy 247

For the Younger Scholars 277

About the Author 289

Foreword

Pastor Dave Russell

The foreword of a book is like the cellophane that is wrapped around a box of candy. You do everything you can to tear that stuff off the box as fast as you can so you can get at the goodies. And you know, that awful stuff can be so hard to tear off! Sometimes it takes your fingernails and your teeth to get after it. But on occasion the cellophane has important things printed on it. Maybe it says, "On Sale!" Or maybe "New Flavors!" So, Forewords to books might be helpful even though we want to get to the goodies that follow as fast as we can.

So, my first admonition is to slow down. What follows are words actually spoken by Walter Cross in various lessons and sermons. It might even be a good idea to read them out loud. You will want to savor these little morsels, not just gobble them up.

When you lift the lid on a chocolate box you see a whole array of shapes, sizes and colors. My absolute favorite is the chocolate covered caramels and I know how to spot them! They are always perfectly square. But I would tire of them if there were no variety. Walter has provided us with a lot of variety in these pages. There are lighthearted stories told only as Walter can tell them. There are deep theological truths that are covered with

graceful, grandfatherly explanations that make these truths go down so easily.

Toward the back of the book, Walter has included some Christmas treats for the kids. But don't be fooled; you will find them delectable, too. We all sneak the kids' candy from time to time, don't we?

Perhaps this book is so endearing because Walter connects with the child that is still alive and well in our souls. He is a master storyteller! He takes sound doctrine and teaches it through stories so that our childlike minds can grasp them. Walter learned a very important lesson from his grandmother. She would bake cookies when he would come to visit. And she knew that sometime during the night, Little Walter would sneak into the kitchen in search of some of those cookies. And being the kind grandmother she was, she would always leave out three of them on a low shelf where he could get at them. And Walter has done the same for us. This has been his lifelong practice when he preaches: he has put the sweets down low where we can get at them and savor them.

You may be a person who likes to read the deep thoughts of theologians throughout history. You may like to read the scriptures in their original languages. You may like to listen to the world's foremost preachers on the Internet. You may like to immerse yourself in Christian philosophy. All that is fine and good. But Jesus the Christ made His truths understandable through simple stories. Why? Because the gospel is simple. Salvation is simple. And the Word is sweet... like honey on your cornbread.

In the genre of devotionals, *Sweet Samples from Scripture* will be read by saints well into the future. And like us, they will nod their heads, chuckle, laugh out loud, tear up and ponder. They will be reminded of the old hymn, "Oh, the Sweet, Sweet Love of Jesus."

Oh, I know how tempting it will be to read the first entry and want to go on to the next one. But let it settle in for today and enjoy the next one tomorrow.

On a personal note: It is a true honor for me to write this Foreword. I feel like I am handling something holy. But more than that I am giddy whenever I can introduce Walter to my friends. The highest honor you can pay a man is to share him with your friends. So friends, get to know this man, Walter Cross. Be blessed.

David G. Russell
Associate Pastor, Fellowship Church
Knoxville Tennessee

Pastor Walter Henry Cross

Year End and Birth of Christ

Sweet Samples from Scripture

Pastor Walter Henry Cross

Is God Preparing You?

Luke 1:76-80:

⁷⁶ And you, child, will be called the prophet of the Most High; for you will go before the Lord to prepare his ways, ⁷⁷ to give knowledge of salvation to his people in the forgiveness of their sins, ⁷⁸ because of the tender mercy of our God, whereby the sunrise shall visit us from on high ⁷⁹ to give light to those who sit in darkness and in the shadow of death, to guide our feet into the way of peace. ⁸⁰ And the child grew and became strong in spirit, and he was in the wilderness until the day of his public appearance to Israel.

Today we're talking about John the Baptizer, and I use that word on purpose because some of our Bibles say John the Baptist. That's not an error, but it can be misconstrued as John belonging to a certain denomination. That part's not true. But John's function, one of his many, was to baptize people into the body of Jesus Christ. Not so much in the Jordan River but into a new way of thinking. And that word baptize means to cover or submerge or to be sprinkled, in some cases, or to be poured, but the best word is cover.

In the first chapter of Luke, let's go down to verse 76. *And you O child*, the child here is John. And this is his assignment, this is his prophetic purpose: *will be called the prophet of the Most High*. John's title and function is a prophet and the word prophet in this sense means a foreteller of the truth, not a forecaster saying if it's going to rain tomorrow or snow next week. John's role was to tell the truth as God told him, and what was the purpose of this truth, and where it was going.

Now the source of the truth was the Most High God; we've got that right in Scripture.

For you will go before the Lord. The Lord here is Jesus Christ and that's where we get the term forerunner. John was a forerunner. Back in those days they didn't have late-breaking news, they didn't have those little things that will flash on your phone or flash on your television to tell you something of importance was going to happen or was taking place. Instead, there was a person called a herald. A herald would run into town, sometimes blow a horn, and then tell the people what the king wanted them to know. John was a type of herald. His function was to go before Jesus and tell the news or, in other words, to introduce Jesus to the people.

Now, let's see how this went. *For you will go before the Lord to prepare* — John's purpose was to prepare — *to prepare the way.* The way of Jesus was going be difficult because the society in which John's ministry and Jesus' ministry was to take place was anti-messiah. The religious elite, the Sadducees, Pharisees, scribes, and all the rest, were not wanting a messiah to come and destroy their way of doing things. They were trying to convince the people that they were their only hope of salvation. Now, John is saying something different. He's going to *prepare the way of the Lord.*

Let's look at verse 77. *To give knowledge,* because people perish without knowledge. John was a purveyor of information. He was saying: It's time to be saved. Now that's an interesting concept. When John talked about repentance, the people had been put under the tyranny of the religious elite. They were being told that repentance was not possible unless they paid for it with all sorts of financial or animal sacrifices and rituals. So the people were often depressed, especially if they didn't have money to pay for that particular type of sacrifice that they needed.

But John is saying something different. He's saying, I'm preparing you. I'm giving you the information; this information

will lead to your salvation without the aid of the priest or the high priest. And of course, this caused confusion. John was announcing to the people of God a way to salvation and forgiveness for their sin. Before, forgiveness was not possible without the intervention of a priest which also had a financial component to it. You had to pay for it. Much later in history, but still a long time ago, Martin Luther, said the same thing, when he put those theses on the door. He was saying, I don't see why we have to pay for the forgiveness of sin, it's right here in the Bible.

Let's look at verse 78. *Because of the tender mercies of our God.* God is merciful. Ask me, ask your neighbor and ask the class, how has God shown mercy in your life? He is merciful. He has not given us an invoice and held us to the sin debt that we owe. *Whereby the sunrise shall visit us from on high,* that would be Jesus Christ. It says sun here, s-u-n, but you can put s-o-n there because he's rising up as we move toward Christmas morning. He is rising up in our in our lives and he's like the sun, he's our light.

So, don't get mad when in Dollywood they said "We've got a million lights." Jesus is our light. I enjoy the lights on the side of the road, on the front porches, in the bushes, on the Christmas trees. I don't get angry when people put candles in the window because it just reminds me that Jesus is the light of the world. What makes me sad is when they take them down because Jesus is the light every day, not just at Christmas time.

A light to those who are sitting in darkness. They were sitting in darkness because they were uninformed. Sometimes the powers that be have a need to keep the masses of the people uninformed so the people cannot make wise decisions.

And in the shadow of death. Death was a tyranny. For us, death is a stepping-stone, it's our exit ramp into a fuller life with Christ, but at that time it was so dark and so unknown that the people really feared and dreaded death.

To guide our feet into ways of peace. Don't we need that? We are seeking for peace, you know, for change in our neighborhoods. We long for peace and change in our families and our churches and mainly in our own hearts. John came to guide us to Jesus who's going to take us to peace.

Verse 80, *and the child grew and became strong.* He was raised like someone who has taken a Nazarite vow. The Nazarites were a group of people who dedicated themselves. They were monastic, which means that they lived apart, and they spent their time dwelling on the things of God. They didn't even shave and there's nothing significant about that except they were separated from the rest of the public to prepare themselves for just for this particular moment.

And he was in the wilderness unto the day of his public appearance. God took him to be away by himself. You know, you go off to school, you go off to another place in school, sometimes that's like a wilderness, but it's also a place of preparation. It's also a place of development. It's also a place where you can hear wise wisdom from those who have gone before you. John's teacher was God himself, and God took him to a place apart, where he would not be interfered with, and where he would not be confused by the sounds of the city. Where he would not be disturbed, or upset about what was going on around him. John had a single focus and his single focus, readers, was to prepare the way of the Lord.

Something to think about is to identify where in your life the mercy of God has made the difference. Think about that. Also think about times in your life God has used for preparation, where God has taken you aside. It may have been something that was happening at work, it may have been something that was difficult. During that season, God was preparing you for something else.

Pastor Walter Henry Cross

Our Package Has Arrived

¹⁰ But the angel said to them, "Do not be afraid. I bring you good news that will cause great joy for all the people. ¹¹ Today in the town of David a Savior has been born to you; he is the Messiah, the Lord. ¹² This will be a sign to you: You will find a baby wrapped in cloths and lying in a manger."

Luke 2:10 - 12

We're going to take a look at the nativity scene this morning and we are going to look at some of the elements there that sometimes we tend to overlook, though we get a glimpse of them in some of our carols. And when we read or recite Luke 2, it reminds us of the nativity scene that we see in so many yards and on billboards around the area this time of year. Everything there is very significant, especially the baby Jesus.

Now, I want to share with you something that happens to me. I order a lot of stuff online and I have an app on my phone that notifies me when my package is delivered. It says, Your package has arrived. Well, if it's something that I'm really, really anxious to get, that gets me excited. I know I need to go and open the front door or go home the quickest route to get my package. What I want to share with you this morning is that our package has arrived and it's being announced in several ways.

We like getting the notification on our phones, but what about the angels? The Bible says that the angels said - we often say that the angels did sing and I don't think that's much of a discrepancy - but they brought forth an announcement whether it was melodic, or had harmony, or was just a recitation. It's

the information that's important, and the information that the angels brought forth was that Jesus the Messiah, the savior of the world, had arrived. So that's why we often see these beautiful angels in the nativity scene around Christmastime. They are telling us, as they told the shepherds, that our package has arrived.

Now what about the shepherds? Why shepherds? Jesus, as a king, could have been born in a palace. He could have been born in opulence. He could have been born with riches, but he was not. He was born in a place that's lowly, where the animals received their nutrition. So, why the shepherds? The shepherds also were of low estate. They were put away, ostracized, from the general population because of a certain aroma that sheep and sheep herders had. It was unpleasant and it irritated other livestock and offended a lot of people, so they were not people of status in the community. Now their product, the meat and wool that they would get from the animals, was very, very, very well received, but the shepherds themselves were not. Well, God chose to make his announcement by the angels to the shepherds in the field and told the shepherds, their long awaited Savior, their King, their package — had arrived. The same is true for us today. Your package has arrived.

… their long awaited Savior, their King, their package – had arrived. The same is true for us today. Your package has arrived.

We also see standing around the manger two very interesting people. We see Mary, a young mother, and we see Joseph. We see Mary, who had a direct connection to the throne of David on earth. It has been predicted by the prophets that the savior

would come through the line of Jesse, which would be David and David's throne, so we know she's special. Joseph also had an indirect line to the throne of David, but he was special because he was obedient to the voice of the angel. The angel had told him that he had a package coming and this morning the angel told him his package had arrived.

Now who else do we see gathered around the nativity scene? What about about the three wise men? They were not at the manger when Jesus was born, although a lot of manger scenes artistically put them there. But there's one truth about them, they were given a star, like the stars we put on top of our Christmas trees and put in our windows, a guiding star. The purpose of the star was to tell them that they had a package coming and to tell them that the package had arrived. And of course, they went down into Egypt to find Jesus about two years later, and worship him there.

This Christmas morning, where do we find Jesus? He's not under the Christmas tree, but he is in our hearts.

The manger scene itself is telling us this morning that Jesus Christ has arrived. Our package has arrived. Now we need to pick it up, we need to open up the Word of God, open up our hearts, and put Jesus in there. There's something I always say this time of year and I want you to think of this as you ponder and wonder about the glory of the birth of Jesus, Emmanuel. God is with us. There are some places that we look for Jesus but he's not there. He's not away in the manger any longer, the manger is empty. He's not on a cruel Roman cross, the cross is empty. He's not in the garden tomb, the tomb is empty. This Christmas morning, where do we find Jesus? He's not under

the Christmas tree, but he is in our hearts. So, think of this and discuss it today as you celebrate Christmas. Where do we find Christ today? How can we involve Christ on this, his birthday? As we celebrate with worship and with our friends, let's keep Christ first. And remember, your package has arrived.

Pastor Walter Henry Cross

Next Stop Bethlehem

¹ Now muster your troops, O daughter of troops; siege is laid against us; with a rod they strike the judge of Israel on the cheek. ² But you, O Bethlehem Ephrathah, who are too little to be among the clans of Judah, from you shall come forth for me one who is to be ruler in Israel, whose coming forth is from of old, from ancient days.

Micah 5:1-2 ESV

There's a special journey that we take each year. Beginning at Thanksgiving, we start heading back to Bethlehem. It's a journey of joy and it's a journey of difficulty. Sometimes we're in the valley, and sometimes we look up over the mountain tops. Let's see what the Lord has in store for us today through one of the prophets in the Old Testament by the name of Micah.

Now the Old Testament is the previous contract of God's promises. You'll remember that in Romans we found out that the promises in the Old Covenant or the Old Testament are still sacred, even though we are dealing in New Testament realities in this Advent season as we move toward Christmas. We can find the essence of the birth of Christ in the Old Testament.

Now muster, your troops, O daughter of troops — that's the nation of Israel — and that's me and you today. *Siege is laid against us* in the community where we live and where we worship. Here in Knoxville, that means the communities of Lonsdale, Mechanicsville, East Knoxville, and so forth. For others reading this, that also means the city, county, and nation where you live.

The powers of darkness have laid siege against us and the troops of the enemy are marching against us.

But you, O Bethlehem Ephrathah — that word means fruitful — listen to what the word says about Bethlehem: you are too small, your land mass is too small. You are so insignificant. You are the one the troops will run over. You are the one that nothing good can come out of. You are the one who is not important. You are not big, you are not New York City or Atlanta. You are so small that the powers of this world don't even count you. It's talking about us, our own little neighborhood.

But wait a minute, are we so small that when our children die, it's not important? Are we so small that when we complain about our streets, it gets ignored? Are we so insignificant that when they redevelop other areas, the city ignores us?

Well, let's see what the Bible says. It goes on to say, you're so small, you're so insignificant compared to your brothers and sisters; they have larger territory, they have more powerful armies; they are stronger, they have more ability and more resources. But from you will come forth one who will rule Israel for God.

I was standing in LAX International Airport, in front of a board that had the schedule of arrivals and departures, and I was trying to get back home the best way I knew how. Everywhere on that schedule, anywhere close to my home in East Tennessee, was the word: Canceled. See, people were trying to get to Chicago, they were trying to get to Atlanta, they were trying to get to Miami, they were trying to get to New York City, Paris, and London. And my hometown in Tennessee was so insignificant compared to those other cities that every time they got a plane they could fill up with these other destinations, they would cancel mine. I kept standing there until a person told me to turn in my ticket and fly standby. They couldn't guarantee where I was going but they would make a connection and get me home quicker. I turned in my ticket and I waited. I waited

like you all have been waiting since Thanksgiving. I waited for one hour, then two hours, and three hours, and four hours. Then, there was an announcement. The announcement said Gate 8 boarding for Memphis, Tennessee, with a connecting flight to Charlotte, North Carolina, and an ending flight destination of Chattanooga, and I knew I was almost home.

We've been on a journey for a while; we've been going back to Bethlehem. We've been moving away from the mall, away from the hype, and away from the men in red suits — all minor issues. We've been moving back to the majors. We've crossed mountains, we've gone through valleys of despair, and now we're almost home. We're almost beside the manger that introduces us to a baby born in a small place that's going to do big things.

You may think that you're worshipping in a very insignificant place, but God told me to tell you that big things are going to come out of you. I'm not talking about somewhere else that seems bigger or more important. I'm talking about right here, and you. Big things are going to happen because Bethlehem Ephrathah means fruitful. Let your roots grow deep, let your sprouts grow up, let your limbs hang over this part of the city. If God dispatches you to some other part of this world, take the love of this place with you, take the power of Christ and go and do the Lord's work.

You're almost to Christmas morning, when Jesus gave a gift. Don't you know it's just the right size, it's just the right price, and it fits my situation well. Let me tell you what I needed. I needed love; I had just run out. I needed mercy: I was empty. I needed grace; all my grace was gone. But one Christmas morning, Jesus was born in a manger and gave me back all the love I ever needed. He gave me back all the grace that I could carry, and he told me that mercy fits my situation.

See, I was born and shaped in iniquity. I wasn't seeing. I was lost and couldn't find my way home, my road to home, my vehicle, my plane, my train, my boat, my car, and even my

heart said cancelled: no destination for me. But Jesus my Savior went to the cross. He said, Walter, you can make it home from the cross.

Don't you know this morning that you can make it home from wherever you are? God may take you from one place to another, but he will bring you home.

Pastor Walter Henry Cross

Sing a New Song

¹ Sing to the LORD a new song; sing to the LORD, all the earth.

² Sing to the LORD, praise his name; proclaim his salvation day after day.

Psalm 33:1-2

It's a new year and today we have a very interesting psalm. We're going to continue the theme that we started in Psalm 33, which is a musical rendition of joy. We're going to continue this idea of exuberant worship. In Psalm 96, the psalmist is writing about preparation for worship and he begins by saying, *Sing a new song, sing unto the Lord a new song.* Isn't that a good thing for a new year?

Now this idea of singing a new song is more involved than just putting forth a melodic vocal expression. It has to do with a new attitude, a new way of thinking, a new mindset, a new beginning. We're talking about singing a new song. We need to quit singing old sad songs. I'm not talking about anything that's in the hymn book. I'm talking about our tendency to whine and to sing sad, sing the blues, and sing about trouble everywhere. And you know, there is trouble everywhere, but why exemplify it? There's trouble in the Middle East, there's trouble in Canada, there's trouble in South America, there's trouble on my street, and sometimes in my home. But I have decided to follow the psalmist, who was a worshipper, and I'm going to sing a new song in this new year.

Now the question comes to mind, why? Why do we need to sing a new song? Why do we need to change up our worship? The

answer comes back very clearly in the 13 verses of this psalm of preparation to worship. First, Jesus has saved us. This is a prophetic psalm. It's talking about the reign of Jesus Christ. He has saved us, so we have security. We live in a time of cyber security where nothing is safe. You can get hacked backward and forward on your devices, but we have celestial security in Jesus Christ. That encourages me to sing a new song. I always tell people, if I ever get hacked, they're going to find out a whole lot about Jesus because that's what I talk about online. We are

> **He has saved us,
> so we have security.**

redeeming the internet for Jesus.

So, sing a new song with exuberance, with energy, and with clarity.

Another reason why we should sing is that people overhear us when we sing a new song. Again, I'm not talking exclusively about a melodic expression, but when we talk, when we walk, our countenance should be in cadence with the harmony of heaven. Therefore, we're singing a new song with our behavior. You've heard of *Whistle a Happy Tune*? When you see someone going down the street or on the bus or doing a job and they're whistling a happy tune, it's because they're happy on the inside. If we're happy about Jesus, we're going to sing a new song in this new year. It's going to come out in our eyes and in our smile. Anybody can look sad, it's not hard. It doesn't take a whole lot of muscle power for someone to be all sad and look like he's soaking in lemon juice. But, if you just smile, everything is different. Now, it's not magic. Stuff isn't going to change overnight or automatically, you know. Your sweetheart may not come back, but Jesus is still on the throne.

That brings us to another point of why we should sing a new

song. Not only is Jesus sovereign, he is worthy of all the praise. The psalmist says all other gods, with a small G, are worthless. They're like a sack of rocks. They may have beautiful artistic designs, but they didn't make the heavens, they didn't make the earth, they did not breathe life into your body. So that's why we can sing a new song. We can sing a song about the vibrance of God. He's real. He's real in the morning, he's real in the afternoon, he's real at night, he is real. He is alive and he is active in our lives, therefore we can sing a new song. We don't have to sing some lowdown blues song about how my baby done left me, and cry. I know you don't drink beer so you'd have to cry in your milk.

Another reason to sing a new song is because Jesus is coming back. He is coming back to establish order instead of chaos, he's coming back to right every wrong, he's coming back to change this world order to one that is conformed to his will. That ought to get you excited. When you know something good

We can sing a song about the vibrance of God. He's real.

is going to happen, sometimes it just makes you want to sing, makes you want to bust out all over. I sing because I'm happy.

To be joyful on the inside in the midst of a crisis affects yourself and others. Sometimes you can chase the blues away with a song about Jesus. So, think about some songs that lift your spirits. You can look in the hymn book or it could be a song that just talks about being happy. I want you to sing a new song and I want you to think about the songs that bring you joy. You may not be able to carry a tune in a bucket, my hand goes up right there, but you ought to be able to sing a new song. Even if you sing the old songs, like *Amazing Grace* or whatever song the Lord puts on your heart, you can sing it in this new year in a new way. I'm not talking about changing the arrangement.

I'm talking about singing it with more enthusiasm, there's that word again, with more enthusiasm, with a more convincing way of singing your joy. Don't be like a drudge saying, I've got to sing the same old song again but sing because you're happy, because you're filled with joy.

The God Who Delivers

²⁹ "Lord, now you are letting your servant depart in peace, according to your word; ³⁰ for my eyes have seen your salvation ³¹ that you have prepared in the presence of all peoples, ³² a light for revelation to the Gentiles, and for glory to your people Israel."

Luke 2:29-32

This was spoken by Simeon, a priest of many years who had been given a promise, and this promise was delivered. God had promised him that he would not see death until he saw the salvation of Israel, which was the birth of Messiah who is Jesus Christ.

Let's look at how we got to this point. Go back up a little bit to Luke 1:26 where we see the angel Gabriel coming for the second time to visit a person. First he visited the lady we know as Elizabeth. Now, she was past childbearing age, but Elizabeth and Zacharias found themselves expecting a child. Zacharias didn't believe it and because of his lack of faith, the Lord shut his mouth for the duration of the pregnancy all together. Sometimes the Lord has to shut you up just to get you to listen to him. Zacharias didn't speak again until the day it was necessary for him to name the child. Everybody in the community expected Zacharias to name his child "Jr.", which was common. They didn't use the word "Jr.", but they would use "son of" or use the term "bar." B-a-r, which is the equivalent to our "Jr." on the end of a name, would have been in front, and means "son of." Zacharias would have been culturally correct to name him that, but God told him to name the child John.

That's where we get the Biblical historical figure, John the Baptist, or the more theologically correct term would be John the Baptizer.

Now, if you see someone coming into your life and telling you that miraculous things are going to happen, you are probably going to be at least a little afraid.

Now, back to this second visit of Gabriel's. Elizabeth was expecting and Mary, the Virgin Mary, who we know as one of the figures in the nativity scene, is Elizabeth's cousin, and comes to visit her. They were a great distance apart in age. We think Mary was probably about 14 years old. We don't know how old Elizabeth was, but she was probably on the north side of 65, so her pregnancy was quite a miracle. She could've been as old as 80. And here they were, both expectant mothers. They were both excited about it. They didn't know a whole lot about what was going on, but they knew it was from God. Mary relates the story about her pregnancy and how the same angel, named Gabriel, which means "strength of God," came and spoke to her. Gabriel told Mary she was going to have a child. He's going to be the savior of the world. And he's going to lead Israel. He's going to sit on the seat of David, and all the people of the world are going to make up his kingdom.

There are some things in our scriptures today that let us know that Mary was both human and spiritual. She was afraid. Now, if you see someone coming into your life and telling you that miraculous things are going to happen, you are probably going to be at least a little afraid. That would be natural. But the angel said, Don't be afraid, because you are the favored one, you are the one that God has picked for this particular miracle to happen. And that gave her some calm and some peace about the birth of this precious child.

But an interesting question is, why was Mary afraid? I'll give you some reasons. There was a cultural stigma about being expectant prior to marriage. Because Mary was pregnant, that gave Joseph, her fiancé, the right to kill her or to have her killed, and to leave her. This wouldn't be a scandal on his part but would be on her part and her family because it would indicate she had been with a man during the time that she was engaged to Joseph. Now, that would make you afraid because how are you going to explain this miracle? People still don't believe it today, so you know they had a hard time back then trying to explain it.

Yet the angel said, "Don't be afraid." There are some things that go on in our lives today, miraculous things that we cannot explain, but don't be afraid. There are some things that God is asking us to do that we cannot do without him, but don't be afraid. Don't look at your future as just what might happen, look at it as what God is going to do because God always delivers. He always does what he says he is going to do.

> ## There are some things that God is asking us to do that we cannot do without him, but don't be afraid.

Now, it's that time of year where UPS, FedEx, and the post office are doing their best to deliver packages on time and trying to get them delivered before Christmas Eve. For about the next five weeks, they're going to be busy delivering packages with a promise of getting them there before Christmas. Some are not going to make it. Amazon is going to do their best, but some are just not going to make it. But when God makes you a promise, he always delivers.

Now, don't let your watch or your clock get in the way. You may be looking at the calendar saying, Lord you said you

were going to do this when? You said you were going to do this how? You said you were going to do this but we don't see any evidence of it. When we think like this, what happens? We get frantic, we get nervous, we get fearful, our anxiety level rises, and we become afraid. But when we become afraid, the word comes again just like Gabriel came and said, Don't be afraid. God's got this, and as we approach Christmas morning, we need to keep thinking God has this, he has our back, he is bringing us salvation, that salvation is in Jesus Christ, we're covered under the blood.

Jesus came into our existence, he became Emmanuel. He died to pay for a debt that we owe, that we couldn't pay. Now, why would God send his son to do all of that and then turn around and not fulfill his promise? God always delivers, Jesus always delivers. Whatever he's promised you, he's going to do. God always delivers. You have something to look forward to. Not only Christmas Day, which is going to be a joyous time in the life of our church and in your life and in your families' lives. He always delivers every day for the rest of your life.

Pastor Walter Henry Cross

The Importance of a Promise

Luke is driven to tell the most accurate accounting of the life of Jesus Christ possible. Being a historian and a scientific person, Luke has made a compilation of stories both oral and written so that we have some great information. We've looked at Elizabeth and her miraculous conception beyond the age of childbearing. Now we're going to focus on the coming together of Mary, the mother of Jesus, and Elizabeth, the mother of John, before the birth of Jesus Christ and before the ministry of John.

Have you ever experienced, as you look back over your life, that sinking feeling in your stomach that happens when someone assures you that they're going to do a certain thing a certain way at a certain time and they just don't do it? It may be beyond the scope for them to do, or a misunderstanding of the time or place or what is to be performed. Or you may find out that they just don't care and misinformed you. Whatever the reason, the end result is you have that little sick feeling in the bottom of your stomach when someone does not fulfill their promise.

Sometimes people can't do what you want them to do or what they promised you they were going to do but they come back and tell you. I won't be able to do it today, but I'll do it tomorrow, or I can't do it tonight, but I will first thing in the morning. That's an affirmation of a promise, that is the guarantee of a promise. Now, the promise was to Israel, and to us, that there was going to be a salvation, a change of events, a new government, and a new system. This promise was very

important to the people of Israel. The reason it was important is because they were in bondage, they were in captivity by a foreign occupying government; they had been exiled from their land and now they were prisoners in their own land. Their history, going all the way back to Egypt, gave them the idea that they needed a change and that this was promised all the way back in Abraham's day. Now here's the fulfillment of that promise, so you can imagine why Elizabeth and Mary were so excited.

I want to encourage you to know that out of mystery, out of darkness, and even out of confusion, God can bring a miracle.

Elizabeth lives north of Mary, so Mary prepares herself to make the journey to visit her cousin Elizabeth. Probably she has heard by way of mouth that Elizabeth was expecting. How news traveled there in those days was not by cell phone and newspaper. Usually traveling merchants who knew families that were scattered in different regions of the country would take messages either written or oral. They would say, Did you know what's happening to your cousin? That's one way word got around. Sometimes even the Roman soldiers were kind enough to tell different families what was going on in a different region. Anyway, Mary got the word. Mary went to see her cousin; an older lady and a younger lady.

When Mary got there, Elizabeth greeted her with a celebratory shout. Now, don't let anybody tell you that there wasn't shouting in the Bible. A celebratory shout acclaiming her, affirming her as the woman chosen of God to bring into this world the Savior Jesus the Christ. In kind, Mary affirmed Elizabeth in her pregnancy beyond the physical limitations of

the body and that she was bringing about the one who would be the announcer, the one who would be the pronouncer, the one who would be the trailblazer for Jesus Christ.

These are two happy women, celebrating an unusual situation. They did not know how or why all of this was taking place. It was a strange set of events, but I want to encourage you to know that out of mystery, out of darkness, and even out of confusion, God can bring a miracle. While the miracle was taking place, Elizabeth and Mary were rejoicing. That says something to us this morning. We can rejoice while God is doing his thing. We need to be patient and wait, just like we're waiting for Christmas morning. We need to be patient and wait and praise. We can praise while we're waiting for the fulfillment of the promise.

Whatever the problem is, whatever the situation is, go ahead and praise God.

When the angel Gabriel visited Mary, he delivered the affirmation of things to come, the promise to be fulfilled. Sometimes we think that God is running late, but we know that's wrong, don't we? We get a little impatient. But we need to affirm each other and reassure each other that the Lord God Almighty is on his way. Not only to Bethlehem, not only on December 25th, Christmas morning, but he's on his way to whatever's going on in your life. Whatever the problem is, whatever the situation is, go ahead and praise God. Whatever the tragedy is, whatever is going on either right or wrong in your life, the Bible says to give thanks in all things. If you do that, you'll have a blessed life. Mary sang a song, a beautiful song that revealed that she knew even at a young age the promises

of God. She knew what had happened down in Egypt. She knew about what went on in the wilderness. She knew what was going on in her life. And she knew that one day there would be a savior that would take the world away from sin.

You'd be surprised what you can go through when you realize what you already know. Something to think about is what do you do while you're waiting on God? How can you lower your anxiety level while you are waiting on God's promise? How do you know the promises of God? How do you know what to wait for? What is God revealing to you now in this present time? What is God sharing? What hope is there for today and tomorrow and for next year?

Pastor Walter Henry Cross

New Beginnings

Sweet Samples from Scripture

Pastor Walter Henry Cross

Begin With a Note of Praise

¹ Sing joyfully to the LORD, you righteous; it is fitting for the upright to praise him. ² Praise the LORD with the harp; make music to him on the ten-stringed lyre. ³ Sing to him a new song; play skillfully, and shout for joy. ⁴ For the word of the LORD is right and true; he is faithful in all he does. ⁵ The LORD loves righteousness and justice; the earth is full of his unfailing love. ⁶ By the word of the LORD the heavens were made, their starry host by the breath of his mouth. ⁷ He gathers the waters of the sea into jars ; he puts the deep into storehouses.

Psalm 33:1-7

I just want to share some thoughts as we enter this new year. We're crossing over from our Yuletide celebration, and are entering the time of Epiphany, a time of new beginnings. Very shortly, we'll be on our way to our time of celebrating the resurrection. My, doesn't the calendar move. But while it's moving, we can slow it down just long enough to praise the Lord. And that's what we're going to talk about today.

Let's look at Psalm 33, which starts off very exuberantly. We believe that David had a lot of input in the first forty Psalms and they were psalms of celebration, songs of praise. Now, we understand from King David's life that he'd been through a whole lot. He had to escape his palace because his life was being threatened by his own family. He was hunted down by the previous king. He had spears thrown at him. He experienced revolt and all types of turbulence in his kingdom.

He was a man of war and violence and that violence crept into his own household. So, David was a man who had a lot to contemplate and to reflect upon. But in these Psalms of joy and praise he decided that God was worthy of all the praise. He starts off on a high note and that's where we ought to start this year off, on a high note. We don't need to drag all that baggage in from last year. Last year is gone. The new year is here. Praise the Lord for another year. Shout for joy to the Lord and raise your voice in praise.

Now you may say that your demeanor is just not like that, you're not that type of person, you're a quiet person, you don't make a whole lot of noise. But I guarantee you if the Publishers Clearing House showed up at your door in the next few minutes with twenty-five million dollars, there's a good possibility you would shout for joy. Well, the Lord gives us breath every day, which is something beyond price, so it's okay to be exuberant in whatever mode of expression you use, and to be excited about the presence of the Lord.

This psalm is addressed to the righteous because people who are not righteous don't have a thing to shout for. They are sad and they are thinking about all the evil in the world. Their focus is on the evil because they have nowhere to go, no one to turn to. But if we are among the righteous, we have the Lord, so we can shout for joy. We can praise Him in the morning and in the evening and all day long. If we are among the upright, we see beyond the headlines, we see beyond the things that come into life that bring sadness and gloom and doom and woe-is-me. We see beyond that because of our position in Christ Jesus. Give thanks. We always have a reason to give thanks — not just in the latter part of November — we always have a reason. The righteous always have a reason to give thanks to the Lord.

Today's scripture is asking us to focus on the creativeness of God — the world, the trees, the ocean. It goes on to say that the Lord has the ability to gather water up and stack it up the way we stack wheat up. We don't have the ability to stack water

because we're not God. God also has the hidden places of the deep, caverns of water, more than we can ever consume. The next time you hear the headlines talk about a drought, and this will surely happen, just remember that God has all the water in the world. He has all the water we need Again, we're talking about the righteous, the upright, those who have chosen to align themselves with the power of Almighty God.

We can praise Him in the morning and in the evening and all day long.

Now, I'm going to share something with you that's been very helpful to me and I think it might be helpful to you. When you see this world crowding in on you, when you see your space in this world getting a little too small, when you find out that your room — the four walls of your room — are beginning to come in on you, when there's crisis after crisis, when there's difficulty after difficulty, when there's problem after problem, when there's foul attitude after foul attitude, I want you to do something. I want you to go out and appreciate the creativeness of God. Now it's wintertime, so we might have to put a jacket or a coat on, but that's okay. There are still marvelous things that you can find when you go out and look at what God has done. In the wintertime, when the trees don't have any leaves on them, they're not quite as beautiful, unless you begin to look closely at how God has taken those branches and has woven them into an intricate, non-repeating pattern. That's creativity, that's artistry, that's the divine creativity of God.

And if you think for a moment, God designed that tree, he designed every tree in this forest, every tree on my street, every tree in my front yard or back yard, every blade of grass, every bush. God has a blueprint, he designed it all, and he made me. And of all that he created, he decided to put his breath, his *pneuma*, his power of life in me. I can say, Thank you Jesus. I

can say, Praise the Lord. I can say, Praise the king in this new year. I want you to praise God for the things that he's done in your life that you know no man could do, and then shout for joy, give thanks, and praise the Lord in this new year of your life. Let's begin this year on a praise note and keep it going all year long.

Pastor Walter Henry Cross

God Provides

¹ Praise is due to you, O God, in Zion, and to you shall vows be performed. ² O you who hear prayer, to you shall all flesh come. ³ When iniquities prevail against me, you atone for our transgressions. ⁴ Blessed is the one you choose and bring near, to dwell in your courts! We shall be satisfied with the goodness of your house, the holiness of your temple! ⁵ By awesome deeds you answer us with righteousness, O God of our salvation, the hope of all the ends of the earth and of the farthest seas;

Psalm 65:1-5 ESV

Psalm 65 is a psalm that celebrates the provision of Almighty God. Now to be one who provides, there are some elements that you have to possess. One of the things that the psalm brings out is that God is able. He's powerful. He is sufficient. Something to bear in mind is that in order for someone to provide, to protect, to enable you, you have to know that he has that ability. God is the all-sufficient one. He has the capability to provide, and when we know that, the end result of that knowledge is praise and celebration. God can, he has, and he will provide.

The psalmist here may have been David. Or, it may have been someone who admired David and affixed his name to this psalm and wrote in the style of David. Or, it could have been David writing prophetically, which meant ahead of his time. The psalm starts off by saying *praise is due you*. We owe a debt of praise to the Lord. Praise is our work. Praise is our responsibility. And praise should be our natural response to knowing that

God is able. This is addressed to Zion. Zion is both a place and a people. Zion is both Israel and me and you. So, we owe God praise for all that he's done.

The psalmist goes on to say that we should perform our vows. That's liturgy, the work of the people. It may be as formal as an affirmation of faith during our worship service. By the way, you can do this during the week. You don't have to wait until you go to your houses of worship to affirm the presence and the power of Almighty God. It could be something as simple as saying, Amen. Amen means I agree with what was just said. So, we are to perform our vows, and the reason that we do that in our worship times and worship experiences is because we are aware that God is able to provide.

God hears our prayer. That's another reason to praise the Lord, he hears us.

God hears our prayer. That's another reason to praise the Lord, he hears us. Now, don't get confused. Sometimes we only want to praise the Lord when he answers our prayers in the way that we want them answered. Then we'll come up with a thank you, Jesus. But he always hears us. When I was coming along, my mother would bake some cookies. Oh, wonderful, wonderful cookies. She'd use that Watkins vanilla extract, and you know the Watkins imitation was better than the real stuff. And it would just perfume the house with this wonderful appetizing aroma. Then she would put the cookies out on her little cooling tray and the word would go forth: you can't have any until after dinner. I thought that was a type of torture. I didn't know what to do with all that and sometimes I would venture to ask for a cookie. Sometimes I'd get a No, but most of the time I didn't get any response, and I would venture to ask again. Then my mother would say something that carried a lot of weight with me. She said, "I heard you the first time." Well you know what

that meant, that meant don't ask anymore. But sometimes I would get grace, if a cookie came out malformed, she would break that up and give me a piece. Don't ever think that God didn't hear you.

Sometimes we base our relationship with God on how he answers our prayers. I want you to begin to base your idea of the character of God on the fact that he always hears you. Sometimes his answer is no. Sometimes his answer is yes. Sometimes his answer is, let's wait on that one a while, not yet. The psalmist says he is our provider who always hears us and because of that we should praise Him.

He even hears us when we are in sin, our *iniquities* it calls it in your Bibles, and he forgives us.

That's another act of a provider. Only a provider who has the power of God can forgive sin. You need to know that. Only an all-powerful God — and our God is the only one who is all-powerful — has this power. Through the finished work of Calvary, the gift of his son, he has the power to forgive us. Just know that.

God provides through nature, the bounty of the land, the bounty of the harvest, the beauty of the vistas and the valleys and the skies. That's a testimony from God of his awesomeness. It takes a mighty good God to eradicate sin in my life and when I look at the mountains, when I look at the valleys, when I look at the rivers, when I look at the falls, I understand how big a God he is, and I get confidence from his hugeness because my sins are many. And when I approach with repentance and pray the prayer of forgiveness, he hears me.

The psalmist also goes on to say that he answers our prayers. Not only does he hear, but he answers. He provides forgiveness. He provides enough-ness, the bounty of our table and our life. Most of all, he provided Jesus Christ. God is truly all I need. I want to suggest you rehearse openly the provision of God. What has God done for you lately? What has God provided for you

that you couldn't get at the bank, that you couldn't get at the emergency room, that you couldn't get in your doctor's office, that you couldn't get over the counter, a drug or a prescription — but God and God alone has provided and taken care of you. Tell yourself, He's all I need. He's the all-sufficient one. He's more than enough. He's abundant and my response to that is hallelujah, praise God, the one who provides. Think about how God has provided for you in a way that no one else could have or would have or chose to do, and pause and take a moment to celebrate that. Remember, praise is due him. Why? Because he has, he is, and he will provide just for you.

Pastor Walter Henry Cross

Let God Put Your Life in Order

¹ Bless the LORD, O my soul! O LORD my God, you are very great! You are clothed with splendor and majesty,

³³ I will sing to the LORD as long as I live; I will sing praise to my God while I have being.

Psalm 104:1,33 ESV

We have to be careful this time of year as we enter into what is known as the winter doldrums. The sky is grey, the nights are long, the holidays are over, there are no leaves on the trees, the grass is brown, and we can slip into a little bit of sadness. That's what makes it so wonderful about the scripture that we'll be looking at this morning. The scripture is Psalm 104, a beautiful poetic rendering, possibly written by the Shepherd King, David. We don't know for sure that he wrote it, but it sounds like him. It starts off with a celebration, and often when he would write he would include praise and worship in his writings. One thing that we do know about him is that in his Psalms, in his poetic or melodic expressions, he would talk about his complaint; what was going wrong in his life or with his family or with the war if he was engaged in war or with the country, the nation of Israel. And he would also be very careful to talk about his confession, his personal sin. We can learn a lot from that. He always ended up with praise. In this psalm he ends up with praise, but he's also starting with praise, so we have a praise sandwich.

He talks about how marvelous and how wonderful the Lord is. He uses the metaphor of God dressing himself in beauty as he talks about the majesty of the Lord. He stretches that metaphor into the area of creation. He talks about how the Lord has flung the skies into existence, how he's hollowed out the riverbeds and the ocean floor, how he has suspended the heavens. He talks about the wonder of creation. A very necessary thing for us to get in this psalm is the details. The psalmist is very detailed about God in creation. It is very important. Notice the detail that God has orchestrated, from the huge animals in the ocean to the ants that scamper along the ground, and everything in between. God is a God of great detail.

Then the psalmist talks about order. Order is very important. The opposite of order is chaos. He talks about how God has designed the world to sustain itself. Yes, God was into sustainability before a lot of us caught on to the fact that we were messing up God's world. So God was very involved in sustainability. The animals had something to eat, he had a design for the herb gardens, he had a design for plants and for all of creation. And don't forget the fact that he did all of this with a big helping of beauty. It's just lovely to look at.

God is a God of great detail.

God was a master in design, a master in order, and he also was a master of authority. He was in charge. The psalmist said that he would speak to the mountains and they would scamper away, or he would call them, and they would come to him. He would touch the mountains and they would smoke. All of this gives an indication of the authority of God.

Now, let's apply this. When your life is out of order, in chaos, you need to know the God of order. Look around you. Look at the order that God has put in place. Then go to God and ask

God to put your life in order. Look at God's creative spirit. He is still creating. If you think your life is dull and boring, go to God. Let him create a beautiful life full of majesty, wonder and awe through your belief in Jesus Christ. God will do that for you. Let God be in charge. Let him be the chief administrator of your life. Let him call to you what he wants you to have, let him send away from you what he does not want you to have. Let him be the lord of your life. We can learn so much from the psalmist who starts this psalm with praise. Oh, how wonderful, oh, how majestic is our Lord. He is still the same way.

When your life is out of order, in chaos, you need to know the God of order.

Now, if your life is missing the details, go to God. We don't need to skip the details in our life. Let me tell you why. Every little thing you do is important. There's no such thing as a small sin. All sins transgress the will of God, so we need to deal with them. We need to keep short accounts. The details are important. We don't need to slough over the details in relationships. And we don't need to slough over the details in our Bible study. We don't need to just miss the details and be sloppy and unconcerned. God is a God of details and we need to be very detailed in our lives.

I want you to think about what you have learned from nature that you can apply to your life. Such as, think about how the seasons change, and how that's for a purpose. Are there seasons to life and do they change? What would be the purpose of those changes? What would be appropriate for different seasons of life? Think about this. One of the wonderful things about the creative spirit of God is that even in the seasons the world is always renewing itself. If mankind, humankind, would let it, it always renews itself. The leaves fall from the tree, they

become fertilizer, they nourish the ground, the tree picks up the substance, and you have new leaves the next year. We should be coming new all the time because we are created by a holy God and he keeps on making us new, okay? So, get the details in your life right. God is the authority in your life. He's the power force. God is the one who brings order to your life. As a result of all that, let's just praise him.

Pastor Walter Henry Cross

You Are Invited

¹ Praise the LORD! Praise the LORD from the heavens; praise him in the heights!

Psalm 148:1 ESV

Our reading is in Psalm 148, and we're going to talk about praising the Lord. Not too long from now, when springtime arrives, we're going to have opportunities to be invited to a lot of different functions like weddings, class reunions and family reunions. We're going to be invited to participate in special services that we go to only by invitation like graduations and anniversary celebrations. All these marvelous times, and all by invitation only. Well, today we have an invitation. It's an invitation to praise the Lord. First, the psalmist extends an invitation to the entire heavenly host, all of the created entities of heaven: Praise the Lord, praise the Lord in the highest, all the angels and all the heavenly hosts. Then he moves on to the created atmosphere which would be the moon, the stars, the sun, everything that twinkles by night: Praise the Lord. Then he moves on again to the earth, inviting all of the creation of the earth to join together in a great symphony of praise: the crescendo of the waters hitting the shore, the sound of a river lapping up against the sides of the riverbed, the trumpet of the elephant in the field, the roar of the lion, and the splashing of the sea creatures. All of these things come together to create this great sound and wonder of praise to the Lord.

Then, he stops a minute and tells us why: Because the Lord did it. It's very interesting, the way in which he put it: the Lord created by saying. He said come, and all of the firmament came. He said become, and all of life became. Now, that's a powerful entity. The Lord could say it and it happened. The Lord could order it and it was delivered.

Isn't that wonderful?

We serve an awesome God.

Now, here come more invitations: the man who is the king of a country and his princes, the Queen and her court, people of authority and power in other words, are invited to praise the Lord. And now all the people are invited to praise the Lord. Again, because he is just so worthy. Finally, the last invitation is unfurled and with the sound of many trumpets, the invitation is given to the nation of Israel, God's chosen people. Chosen for what? Chosen why? Why are they special? Because they were assigned to deliver the news of the gospel to the world. Their assignment is still before them and we are engrafted into the Holy Family of God through the sacrifice of Jesus Christ.

We have an invitation, believers, we have an invitation to praise the Lord.

We can do this just by going outside, even at this time of year. We can to observe the vaulted skies, we can see the birds soaring through the air, we can see the blades of grass, and even though they're brown in our region, they're still beautiful, and we can see the barren trees — all giving an indication that God said it and it has been done.

How does that apply to our lives? We serve an awesome God. He's all that and more. He has that power.

A lot of times, in my inquisitive nature, I have asked the Lord, Why? And I've received this response: Because I said so. That's familiar to me because I used to ask my parents that and

sometimes that's all the answer I got: Because I said so. With the Lord and with my parents, that was quite enough because the Lord has that authority and power. And that should bring us comfort. I want to challenge you, to go to the window and look for something that you can praise God for. I want you to observe, as you are driving or walking today, something that you maybe have been passing for years, and praise God for it. We are invited to become a part of this great symphonic rendition of praise. Yes, we're invited to the choir, we're invited to the orchestra. You don't have to sing, and you don't have to play an instrument, but you all can praise the Lord. So, go look and see and talk about the wonders of God. Associate that power, that wonder, that creative beauty to your own life. If God took the time to make the things the way he made them, he took some time to make you and me.

Pastor Walter Henry Cross

Christ Sets Us Free to Live in Harmony

¹ O foolish Galatians! Who has bewitched you? It was before your eyes that Jesus Christ was publicly portrayed as crucified. ² Let me ask you only this: Did you receive the Spirit by works of the law or by hearing with faith? ³ Are you so foolish? Having begun by the Spirit, are you now being perfected by the flesh? ⁴ Did you suffer so many things in vain--if indeed it was in vain?

Galatians 3:1-4 ESV

Let's get into Galatians. Our writer is Paul. Paul is responding to a letter that was sent to him in another location. There was something going on with the church at Galatia that was different than what was happening when Paul was originally there. Paul had been to the church in Galatia and had preached a wonderful revival. People came to the Lord and they began to learn about the new way of Christianity. They were excited about it, they were thrilled about it, it was all new, and the congregations were filling up, and their lifestyle changed. Paul was satisfied and overjoyed with this church and he moved on to another location to do ministry.

Well, while he was away, he received a message that things had changed at the church that he was so proud of. In fact, he got a little upset. He wrote them back and it sounds kind of strong when we get to Galatians chapter 3. He said, "Who fooled you? What happened to you? What is going on? I have received word that you have returned to your former practice of legalism." Now let's talk a little about that. Christianity is about freedom in Christ. One of the important words in

our reading today is the word faith. When Paul taught the Galatians, he taught them to trust in the finished work of Calvary, to believe in Jesus Christ, to confess their sins and live a life of freedom. But some of the more traditional Jewish teachers told them that's too simple, that's too easy, you're getting by, you're sliding by with too much. Sometimes we run into individuals like that in the church today. They want to practice a certain degree of initiation, as if the church or Christianity itself is a club. They want to practice exclusivism, they want to rate people and put them in certain classes or categories because it makes them feel better about themselves.

> **When Paul taught the Galatians, he taught them to trust in the finished work of Calvary, to believe in Jesus Christ, to confess their sins and live a life of freedom.**

But Paul had put away all of those archaic practices and Paul made it very clear in the book of Romans that Jesus did not come to destroy or put away the law, he came to add to the law. The addition to the law carried us to a point of showing us our need for a savior. That savior, of course, is Jesus Christ. Now these teachers were saying that to keep from being disenfranchised with God our Father, we need to work, work, work, work. Now we do need to work in the church, we do need to work in our Christian lives and in our mission fields, but we work because we love Jesus, not because we're trying to work our way to heaven. That has never been so, and it is not the will of God for us to do that. But these teachers evidently gained something personally for pressing down on the people and telling them this new way of Christianity is too simple. They told the people, you need to do something, you need to act a certain way, you need to look a certain way, you need to

obey us. Whenever a man tells you to obey him or whenever a woman tells you to obey her instead of God the Father through Jesus Christ empowered by the person of the Holy Spirit, that's not of God.

Jesus has died for your sin, that debt is paid.

So Paul's upset and he's asking them, because he's like a father who loves his children, What happened to you when I left? You were doing okay, but now you're all messed up. Then Paul tells them to go back to the basics. First, believe in Jesus Christ. Jesus has died for your sin, that debt is paid. Then, live by faith. Then, embrace your baptism. Now the concept of baptism that Paul is teaching has to do with a new way of life. Water baptism is an outward expression of an inward change. So, in the reading, when you run across the phrase, put on new clothes, or being dressed like a person who's following Christ, that's an allusion to baptism. Baptism is when we make a conscious decision to follow Jesus Christ. Baptism actually existed before Christ.

Paul used the illustration that children of slaves and children of the master played together when they were children but as they got older the master awarded his son the inheritance, and the relationship between the slave and the master changed. He is saying that we are like the master's children. The Father, Father Yahweh, Heavenly Father has freed us from the slavery of the law and has given us a righteous inheritance, and we are in the family of God. We are part of the family; we're no longer slaves. We have been taken from slavery to friendship to being the heir. We have the privilege of inheritance.

Paul goes on to say that all of this brings about a type of unity and a type of harmony. Remember when we talked about the creative spirit of God and how he brought harmony out of chaos? We're going to continue that musical metaphor in that God is still the conductor. He's bringing us into harmony. Have you ever been to a symphony? That first five minutes is kind of strange when they're all tuning up their instruments. But when the conductor takes his baton, and he taps the rostrum and the music stand, and they all play that first note, it's all in rich, beautiful, symphonic harmony. We live in harmony. Check your car out. When it's running smooth, it just hums. When it's not running smooth, it clangs and carries on and bubbles and starts and stops. That's the way life is. We need to be in harmony with each other. We need to be in harmony in Jesus. We don't need to look at our differences, we need to look at our similarities in the cross of Jesus.

I want you to think about ways within the body of Christ that we can come together. Come up with some inventive ways for how we can come together as people of God in our churches. Think, what do old people and young people have in common? Christ. What do children and teenagers have in common? Christ. What do people in your community and in your church have in common? Christ. What do people who are non-believers and people who are believers have in common? Christ. So think about ways we can create harmony among all those different people. The answer is Christ.

Pastor Walter Henry Cross

We Are Heirs in Christ

³ In the same way we also, when we were children, were enslaved to the elementary principles of the world. ⁴ But when the fullness of time had come, God sent forth his Son, born of woman, born under the law, ⁵ to redeem those who were under the law, so that we might receive adoption as sons. ⁶ And because you are sons, God has sent the Spirit of his Son into our hearts, crying, "Abba! Father!" ⁷ So you are no longer a slave, but a son, and if a son, then an heir through God.

Galatians 4:3-7 ESV

In today's lesson we are going to talk about chapter 4 of Paul's letter to the Galatians. It's sort of a review of what we went through last time when Paul was saying, O foolish, unwise Galatians, who has put a trick on you, who bought you in, who has convinced you to go back to your previous chains of slavery and sin? Paul uses a lot of words that we can identify with. He uses sin and slavery, how it can confine us, how it can take us down. He also uses the idea of the law restricting our freedom. In today's text, we see Paul explaining to the people why he is so upset about this. He says, I was with you, I was in your homes, I was in your gathering places.

He says, When I was with you, I was preaching the truth the best way I knew how. I was telling you about the freedom in the gospel, how we're free from the chains of sin. You received it, you responded to it, you were excited about it. Then I get this message that you have reverted back because someone else came and they were articulate. They could speak well,

and they gave you a very logical argument. These people that Paul is talking about were called the Judaizers. They were a group of people who considered themselves to be the Church of Abraham and they didn't want things to change. They didn't like change, they didn't embrace change. They thought the law was good enough.

Well, as we've discussed before, Paul was very clear everywhere he went that the law had a function and the function was to show us our need for a savior. That function had been completed. There was a debt and it is logical that the law required a payment, but that payment was made through Jesus Christ and his sacrifice on Calvary. So the puzzling situation for Paul was, why did they revert back to this area of fleshly bondage? He gives an example of when you're the child of the master, you're not even aware of the privilege that you have. You have a lot, but you might as well be a slave. Then he talks about how we have moved from being a child who is treated the same as a slave's child to being the master's child. Why would you choose to go back to something that's confining, that's binding, that's restricting, and that causes guilt and shame?

Paul kept saying the same thing, Why are you going — I'm perplexed. I'm perplexed and I'm upset about this. I'm not mad with you, I'm just loving you and I want to love you back into the kingdom. Paul says, I'm just like a pregnant woman in labor pains trying to birth you back into the kingdom.

There are some interesting concepts that Paul talks about and I'd like for you to think about them. One is adoption. He talks about the legal aspect of our legitimacy as being children of Almighty God. We were adopted, chosen, and that makes us special. You were chosen by God to receive the inheritance that was given to you through Jesus Christ. You were chosen, you were picked out to be blessed. Why would you go back and put on the chains of the world? You are not only a legal heir, but you are a spiritual heir. He gives an interesting example about the slave woman and the free woman. We know about

Hagar and Sarah, and the child of promise and the child born of slavery. One thing we have an opportunity to think about here is why the scripture says put out the woman and the child. What we need to realize is that God did this wonderfully and perfectly. The child of promise was born so that we'd have access to the Father through Jesus Christ, that's all one continuous line. But man, that's me and you, made a detour and decided God was moving too slow and inserted their fleshly idea into the situation and here comes a child born of slavery. We are born of the free woman and it was necessary for God to remove that element out of the home. Now, if you read the scripture in the Old Testament very carefully, you see that God provided for the bondwoman and her child. God said on one occasion, I hear you, your pain, your suffering. On another occasion God said, I see you.

How can we bring this all together for today? I want to ask you the question Paul was asking. Why are you going back? The world wasn't all that much fun to you as you think it was. The world will whisper to you and tell you that those old activities were just wonderful, we miss you around the old watering hole, you don't act like you used to act, you don't do what you used to do, you're just not fun anymore, you're not cool anymore. But I want to tell you I'd rather not be cool and be a part of the family of God then be cool and then get hot later.

Brothers and sisters, why do we make these conscious choices to go back into slavery, to go back into bondage? Now, in my heritage we celebrated Emancipation Day not too long ago. When that news went around the plantation slave camps, there were some older slaves who didn't know another type of life. Some of the younger men and women were anxious to get off the plantation and get on with their lives. But some of the slaves said, How are we going to eat? How are we going to function? We don't have jobs, we don't have money, we don't have food. Some of the younger ones, full of zeal, said we're going to go out and we'll scratch the

land and the Lord will provide. Sometimes it's difficult for us to plow into new ground and that's why we go back to what's familiar. We go back to so-called friends. But you know those friends that pull you away from the Lord and from the church aren't really your friends. They are not the individuals who you need to be associating with.

Why are you going back? You didn't have a good experience the last time. Why are you going back? You did not fulfill the purpose God gave you when you were in that situation. Why are you going back? If he was hateful, mean, and abusive then, if there hasn't been a heart change, he's going to be mean, hateful, and abusive now. If she was stepping out on you then, unless there's been a heart change, she's going to step out on you now. If you were full of sin and addiction and trouble and difficulty then, why would you go back to it now? If it was not the answer then, it's not the answer today. Paul kept pressing this. He kept saying this and he wanted you to know this.

I want you to think about two words, flesh and promises. I want you to look at the idea of the flesh, what has the flesh done for you lately or any time in your life? Let me tell you what I mean when I talk about the flesh. This is our own appetite, our own basic reasoning. It's when the light bulb goes off and you think you have a better idea, but you hadn't consulted God about it and you hadn't prayed about it. That's usually being motivated by the flesh, those natural impulses that we have. I want you to differentiate between being motivated by the flesh and being motivated by the promises in the book of the Lord, the Bible, the holy scripture. Let's be children of the promise and not slaves, not compelled, not chained to flesh and sin.

Pastor Walter Henry Cross

Christ Has Set Us Free to Serve

¹ For freedom Christ has set us free; stand firm therefore, and do not submit again to a yoke of slavery.

⁷ You were running well. Who hindered you from obeying the truth?

¹³ For you were called to freedom, brothers. Only do not use your freedom as an opportunity for the flesh, but through love serve one another.

Galatians 5:1, 7, 13

Valentine's Day is a very special day in the life of the church. The commercial world is full of flowers and candy and special dinners and treats, and all of that is good and wonderful. Even if you can't do anything else but fold over a piece of paper and draw a heart on it and say, Happy Valentine's Day, that is a way of blessing somebody else and letting them know that you really care. Now, part of the history of Valentine's Day goes all the way back to a clergy person who extended love to others even while being incarcerated for trying to be inclusive in the ancient church. You might want to look that up sometime; it's very interesting reading. Yes, Valentine's Day did not come from Walmart, it didn't come from Hallmark, it came from a situation that developed when a clergy person was reaching out to others to be inclusive.

Now we are still in Galatians and studying how Paul was dealing with a very significant situation that developed in the life of the church. Let's review what's going on. Paul is frustrated. He's somewhat upset. We got that from his previous statements when he asked, What has happened to you all?

You were progressing and now you're going back the other way. Then he gave the Galatians some ideas to help them turn around. Repentance is recognizing your situation, recognizing your sinful behaviors and realizing that you need to turn around. Change your mind, change your direction, change your heart, and walk back to the Lord. Wherever you left the Lord, go back. The Lord won't leave you, he won't leave me, but we have a tendency to stray and that gets to the core of what this lesson is about.

Wherever you left the Lord, go back.

Paul had already been in Galatia and he had preached freedom in Christ. Freedom in Christ is the completion of the law. We have learned that the law has a purpose, and that purpose was to outline to us our need for a savior. Now the rules and regulations of the Mosaic code and all the laws of the Old Testament were leading or guiding us to the idea that we needed Jesus Christ in our lives. This started in the Garden of Eden, and continues on up until today. But there were some individuals who were legalistic in their approach to Christian living. They were sort of skeptical about this new freedom in Christ. Maybe it was too easy, they thought. Maybe people would get by with too much. Rules and regulations were easier to follow. Sometimes rules and regulations are easier for a legalist to follow because they make up the rules as they go. Now, what makes it difficult is for the people who the rules are being imposed upon. For those who are being pushed down and separated from the gatherings in the church and not receiving information like the true scriptures, not being able to decipher the language, and it was an advantage to the legalists to keep certain individuals in the dark so they could have control over them. The threat of annihilation, the threat of hell was the power that they used to control the people. So, they fought this idea that Paul was preaching of complete and total freedom in Christ Jesus.

Unfortunately, there are individuals today who preach a very similar message, a group of do's or don'ts: if you follow my rule, if you follow our rule, if you follow our system, this is what's going to happen. That is considered a works mentality. In our Western thought we tend to think this is fair. How many of you know that Christianity is not necessarily fair? We've been chosen, we have been gifted the freedom of Christ. We cannot merit it, we cannot earn it, it's not a paycheck, it is a blessed gift. But still we have the idea in our mind that we need to work toward salvation. We don't need to work to be saved, we need to work because we're saved. Salvation is built on belief in Jesus Christ and nothing else. He is the only one that can eliminate and annihilate sin in our lives. It's not so much what you do, or what you have done, or what you intend to do, Jesus paid it all on Calvary. That's why Paul asked the Galatians, Why are you returning to a system that promised you death? Those of you reading this right now, why have you returned? You've heard the Gospel message, you've celebrated truth, but you're returning to something that did not help you back then.

That brings us to Paul's lesson today included in this chapter Galatians 5 the first 17 verses: do not use your newly found freedom as a right to be abusive.

Sometimes when people are first exposed to new freedom, they just go wild with it. Some teenagers, when they first get that aroma of gasoline and get behind the wheel, they just go wild with it. But with freedom comes responsibility. In the church, we are free to serve. We are also free to not do a lot of things, so we look at that in a kind of reverse way. We're not free to live reckless, but we are free to serve, we are free to live a godly life, we are free to make our lives a testimony. That idea of freedom gives us the possibility of being strong and vital in the church, in the community, and in our homes. You're free not to be abusive, you are free not to be a type of person who will bring down the body of Christ in front of a dying world, but to be a light and to be illuminating. Sometimes guilt and shame and

blame will return us to rules because sometimes we think rules are easier to follow. We think, give me a rule, give me an idea, that way I don't have to think about it. But when you are in Christ Jesus, you are free to live a life that serves others.

Paul kept coming back to that. In order to have a relationship with God the Father through Jesus Christ and empowered by the person of the Holy Spirit, we must have a relationship with our neighbors, our relatives, our friends. I'm not only talking about the person across the street or next-door, but I'm including them in the whole wide world, this neighborhood of creation, this neighborhood of the sea of humanity. We are to do that. We are free to do that.

What freedom do you have that you can utilize to enhance the kingdom? What freedom do you have this morning that you can utilize today to enhance the freedom you've been given? You're free to come in and worship. How's that going to translate into service? You're free to get in your car and go to the supermarket or go to the buffet. During that time, what are you free to do that's going to enhance others? You're going to be in the shopping mall a little bit and maybe you're going to run across someone who has never been told that they are special, that they're unique, maybe just say hello to them. You're free to do that. Don't wait for a response. When there's someone behind you in McDonald's, or there's a car behind you at the drive-through, you're free to say, I'll pay for that meal behind me. You're free to serve. You're free to do all of it. Don't go back, don't turn around, don't give in, don't give out. You may say, Pastor, I've failed. Well, you're free to get up and keep moving forward. You're free to tell the story of Jesus Christ. Enjoy your freedom. Live into your freedom.

Pastor Walter Henry Cross

Two Lists for Life

²⁵ If we live by the Spirit, let us also walk by the Spirit. ²⁶ Let us not become conceited, provoking one another, envying one another.

¹ Brothers, if anyone is caught in any transgression, you who are spiritual should restore him in a spirit of gentleness. Keep watch on yourself, lest you too be tempted.

Galatians 5:25-26 – 6:1 ESV

Let's look at the latter part of the fifth chapter in the beginning of the sixth chapter in Galatians. Paul is still in a very intense struggle with the men and women of Galatia. He's trying to get them to see, to understand, to comprehend that it is not necessary for them to return to the legalism of the past. They should walk in the freedom of Jesus Christ. In our reading today, we see two lists. Paul is just outstanding with his ability to put things in a list and in an itemized fashion. So, he begins to share with the people of Galatia, and those of us who are reading today, the difference between walking in the spirit and walking in the flesh. Now, the law only had the ability to chastise us for things that we have done that were contrary to the will of God; it offered no hope, no redemption. The first list is when Paul tells us to move away from the flesh. How the flesh is defined is that desire, that appetite that we naturally have in our spirit to do anything but the right thing, to go against the grain of God. Sin is actually transgressing against the will of God. And Paul has a list of despicable, ugly, nasty, mean-spirited things that any of us can be found doing if we don't have Christ in the center of our

hearts. Let me share with you a principle that I live by: a man or a woman, a boy or a girl without Jesus Christ in their lives will do anything. This is a this is a hard list. It starts off with immorality and rage. Have you ever shaken your finger at the person at the traffic light ahead of you, you know, pointing up at the sky, trying to get them to see the birds flying over, using that middle finger of your hand? All that kind of stuff is outside of the will of God. Cheating, defrauding each other, breaking harmony, disunity, division, and an explosive temper. Sometimes we say, Well I just have a bad temper. Now, if you are aware of that, half the work is done. You need to give that bad temper to a very good God. God can handle that.

You need to give that bad temper to a very good God.

Then there's another list. The other list is the fruit of the Spirit. Now, I want you to notice that the fruit of the Spirit is not plural. It's not like Walmart, it's not like going to Kroger or to some other grocery store where you can pick this, that, or the other; get some grapes and skip the bananas and get an apple and skip the orange and then get something else. No. The fruit of the Spirit is a changed life that is moving away from fleshly appetites and all of the stuff that's negative and moving toward walking in the Spirit. Don't say, I can handle this one, but I can't do the other one. Or I can love but I'm not always full of joy. Jesus died for our sin. We can claim victory over each aspect of our fleshliness, our worldliness, our sin.

Now let's look at the beginning part of chapter six. Paul encourages us to walk humbly with God and each other. Restoration and reconciliation is the topic of the first few verses in chapter 6 of Galatians. When someone is in difficulty and they are falling, they're failing, they're not making the mark — sin is missing the mark — then those of us who think we

are more spiritual than others should go to them and help them, pray for them and by all means encourage them. Church discipline is encouragement, it's not a verdict or a penalty. Sometimes we feel too good throwing someone out of church. Sometimes we feel real good chastising someone and shaking our finger in their face.

Well, you see how intense Paul has been with the Galatians. That's because he loved them. Don't you also know how intense the love of God is toward us? He cares for and loves us. Restoration and reconciliation is bringing people back together and bringing people back to the Lord. It's not about who you can exclude or who you can chastise or who you can badmouth. So, read through the fruit of the Spirit. Go through each one of them and think of an example of how you can exemplify the fruit of the Spirit in your life today and every day.

Sweet Samples from Scripture

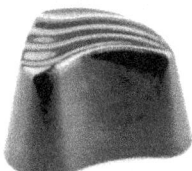

Pastor Walter Henry Cross

Perfect Love

²⁰ if anyone says, "I love God," and hates his brother, he is a liar; for he who does not love his brother whom he has seen cannot love God whom he has not seen.

1 John 4:20 ESV

This is the time of year of Ash Wednesday. You've probably heard about Fat Tuesday, which is a day of decadence in the worldly scene. In the spiritual world, we celebrate Ash Wednesday, which is the beginning of Lent. Ash Wednesday is a time of sorrows, it's a time of reflection, a time of repentance and a time of resolve. Now, it's not so sad because even though we know we are moving toward Calvary, we are also moving toward the resurrection. But there are times in our Christian life where we need to set aside a moment to pause, to reflect upon our sin. You know, when I look at my sin and then I look at the resurrection, I get real happy. When I think about what I have done and what has been done in this evil world and then think of the sacrifice of the Father to send his son to eradicate my sin, I'm happy, I'm pleased, I'm thrilled.

Let's look at the fourth chapter of 1 John. John is the writer. He is an apostle, which means special messenger, one who has been sent. We need to talk about apostles because there are some people today who refer to themselves as apostles. It's okay to have a message sent by God through a modern-day apostle. Your Sunday school teacher is an apostle, your pastor is an apostle because God has sent you a message through them. The

title and the office of apostle don't exist anymore and the reason for that is because we have the entire word of God. So God does not utilize a designated courier to bring us the word but you have access to the word. And an apostle today is someone who is giving us what God would have us to know from his Bible, from the Holy Scriptures.

And an apostle today is someone who is giving us what God would have us to know from his Bible, from the Holy Scriptures.

Now this chapter, as it opens, begins with a very firm statement to separate believers and non-believers, false teachers and real teachers. The criteria is based on belief in Jesus Christ. If someone confesses Jesus Christ as being the son of God, as being the one who has risen from the grave, the one who is both wholly divine and wholly human, who was buried and carried our sins all the way, and, most importantly, who is now ascended and sits on the right hand of the father; if a teacher comes to us teaching that gospel, that good news, that's someone we should listen to. But if they say, Jesus was just a good teacher, you probably need to run away from that. If they say, Jesus was just a good humanitarian, you probably need to run away from that. Anytime they try to limit Jesus from being the son of God, from being all holy, all divine, all human, if they separate that, they're not telling you the whole story and they wouldn't be a teacher sent from God.

The chapter goes on to identify perfect love, complete love. If you can love me and not love my brother or my sister, you can't love God. Or you can love God with all of your heart and you just cannot stand me or someone else in your inner circle, someone in your church, someone in your community, someone on television that you've never met before; your love is incomplete. That word perfect can be defined as completion.

If you have love not for one another but you have love for the Father, your love is incomplete, your love for the Father is faulty. If you have love for the Father and you do not express and act upon the love that you have for your brothers and sisters in Christ, your love is incomplete and your love for the Father is also incomplete. Perfect love loves everybody. I'm going to tell you something that's been helpful for me. A lot of times we have difficulty with an individual and we say, I can't stand them. What we're really talking about is their behavior. But notice this: they are a creation of almighty God and we need to develop a way to love them. You don't have to buy into their behavior. You don't have to accept their behavior. If led by the spirit, you can address the behavior, but that is a holy person in creation. Love them enough to tell them the truth. That's complete love. Don't talk *about* them, talk *to* them. That is complete love. Don't run them down, build them up in the most holy faith. That is complete love.

Anytime they try to limit Jesus from being the son of God, from being all holy, all divine, all human, if they separate that, they're not telling you the whole story and they wouldn't be a teacher sent from God.

Think about the ways that you can use love to build someone up. I'm talking about love that has hands and feet, love that has an anointed mouth. Think about ways that you can love someone in a way that they can tell they're being loved and ways you can build them up in complete love. Unity in the body of Christ is cemented together by love. Express your love for each other and for people you don't even know. How can you do that? You have to ask the power of God to come into you and make me and you a conduit of love.

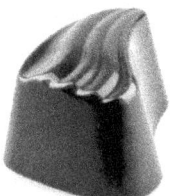

Pastor Walter Henry Cross

But God

¹ As for you, you were dead in your transgressions and sins, ² in which you used to live when you followed the ways of this world and of the ruler of the kingdom of the air, the spirit who is now at work in those who are disobedient. ³ All of us also lived among them at one time, gratifying the cravings of our flesh and following its desires and thoughts. Like the rest, we were by nature deserving of wrath. ⁴ But because of his great love for us, God, who is rich in mercy, ⁵ made us alive with Christ even when we were dead in transgressions—it is by grace you have been saved.

Ephesians 2:1-5 ESV

Let's go into Ephesians. We're going to talk about something that we all are familiar with and that's the word love. We crave love. We are creatures that seek love, we are affirmed by love. We communicate using that word often, but sometimes it's misused and misappropriated. Love that causes physical pain and violence — guess what, that's not love. Now Paul is following up with the church at Ephesus. There has been a great revival there at that church. People have moved out of legalism and out from under the oppression of some of the religious elitists there in the church and in that area, and they are experiencing the freedom of Christ. Any good pastor or teacher will, from time to time, follow up with the new converts, give them a sense of encouragement and remind them of their story. That's what Paul is doing in this second chapter of Ephesians. He started off in the first chapter by reaffirming the supremacy of Christ. We need to know that, and we need to be

reminded of who Christ is — the son of Almighty God. We need to realize how important and significant Christ is in our lives. We need to just know that. We need to hear it. We also need to share it.

Then in the second chapter, he begins to share with them the immenseness of God's love toward us. Now one of the ways that we can identify how much God loved us, and loves us even to this point, is to take a retrospect of our selves; our sin, our depravity, where we were before God entered our lives and before we said, Jesus come into my life come, in today, come in to stay. Do you remember those days? For some of us, it may not have been that long ago. But there should be a point in our lives where there is a remarkable change between what we used to be and where we are now. Now, when we look at that change, we need to look at what we used to be and then see what Christ has done in our behalf.

Let's talk about what he did — he came from glory on the assignment from his Father to take our sins away through the ultimate and supreme sacrifice of the cross. He did it for us. Paul outlines for the Ephesians, and for us today, what we were without Christ. He uses a lot of terms and I'm going to try to break those terms down to one: nothing. Nothing. We were not able to do anything for ourselves. We were lost and nobody was looking for us. We were down and out, we were over and out, we were down for the last count. We were messed up, messed in, messed out, and messed over until Jesus came.

Then Paul uses a phrase that just thrills my soul. He says, *But God*. I want you to sort of relate to a *but God* moment. Is there a *but God* moment in your life? Now that's when you just suppose, you put side by side, the life that you were living prior to Christ and the difference now. There should be a difference, should be a point in your life where there's a difference between the old man or woman and the new spiritual person. A difference between flesh and carnality and walking in the light of Christ.

Now what did love have to do with it? Everything. Love that was so divine, that was compelled to come and see about our condition of sin. Love that was so strong, it was not fickle, it was not the type of love that calls you on Monday and won't call you again until Saturday afternoon to see what you're doing Saturday night. That's not love. God's love energized heaven to the point that Jesus said I'll go and I will be that bridge between the divinity of God and the humanity of mankind. That's love. Love sought me. I can't tell you I was so wise, I was so intelligent, I was so with it that one day I realized I needed Jesus Christ in my life. I was not that smart. What happened? Love arrested me, love wrote me a sentence of eternal life, love bailed me out of hell. Love changed my life, my lifestyle, my conversation, the way I talk, the way I walk. Love did that for me.

Paul is trying to get all of us to realize today how enormous is the power of God's love toward us. So enormous that Jesus died, was crucified, was raised from the dead, and is now in the position of power to continue to love upon us.

You may not be with who you want to be this morning, but you're loved. You may not be where you want to be in your job, but you are loved. You may not have on the threads you think you ought to be wearing, or have a certain address, or a certain type of bank account, or a certain status symbol parked in the parking spot or in the driveway; you may even have to walk to church or your car may be broken down; all of that is involved in this sphere that we call the world, but beside all of that, you are loved. We are loved.

And since we know beyond the shadow of a doubt that God loves us, we need to begin to spread that love abroad. We need to love people in a way that they know that we identify with them. You can't love anybody if you don't feel loved yourself. And love is not a heart-shaped box of chocolates, even though if I could get some I'd eat them, and it's not those aromatic, beautiful roses, even though they're lovely. Love has outgoing

concern for me and you from the throne of heaven through the blood of Jesus Christ and now being empowered by the person of the Holy Spirit. We're in a love affair and there's nothing illicit about it, we are involved and it's alright. I want you to think about the contrast in your life before the *but God* came in. What would have happened, *but God*? What was going on, *but God*? What would be your future, what would be your now, if it was not for that *but God* in your life?

Pastor Walter Henry Cross

Springtime: New Growth

Sweet Samples from Scripture

The Cleansing Love of God

¹ "I am the true vine, and my Father is the gardener. ² He cuts off every branch in me that bears no fruit, while every branch that does bear fruit he prunes so that it will be even more fruitful.

John 15:1-2 ESV

Here we are again at the beginning of spring and at the end of winter. We may still get some snow showers or a blizzard, but spring is coming. Spring brings us today to the scripture in the fifteenth chapter of John, verses 1 through 17. In verse 14 Jesus is telling his disciples that he must go away. They don't want to hear that. They have developed a relationship with Jesus, and they want Jesus to stay around forever. And he tells them that he's not going to leave them by themselves, they will have the power of the person of the Holy Spirit. And he tells them that there are some things he wants them to do. One of those things you will hear in today's lesson over and over again is to abide, to remain.

Jesus uses a springtime metaphor as they were walking along the dusty road. They were headed to the Garden of Gethsemane where Jesus had told them that he was going to be accosted and arrested for crimes that he didn't do, the crimes that we have done, and he might have paused by a whole field of beautiful blossoming vines. These vines were aromatic and it was just a beautiful setting for Jesus to tell the disciples, I want you to stay in the vine, I want you to remain, I want you to stay in the words, the lessons, the examples I have given you.

Then he continues to press the theme about how the work of the Father and the work of the Holy Spirit, and the work of the Son are all together the same and different. That's called a paradox and that's one of the things we're going to understand later, by and by. But today we can understand this: we can understand what Jesus asked us to do. He has asked us to remain, to stay in the vine, to bud, to blossom, and to be fruitful.

Oh, the Father loves us so much, he wants to take away everything that is sucking the life, sucking the energy out of me and you; some things that have clung to us and some things that we are clinging to that just don't mean us any good.

Now, I used to have a little rosebush and that rosebush was accidently stepped on and it divided the plant into two halves. I eventually had to cut away, reluctantly, the half that was weaker to give the stronger half the ability to thrive and to grow. There are some situations in our lives that need to be taken away. In this parable, in this sermon, in this lesson from Jesus, he identifies the Father as the loving caretaker who comes along to do the pruning. The word prune means to cleanse. He comes along to prop us up, to take away, the word that is translated here means to lift up, he comes to lift up our weaker branches off of the ground. He comes to disturb our lives, to cultivate, to dig around the root system to get those nutrients and oxygen in there so we can grow and thrive. And Jesus encourages us to remain in the vine, to remain in his teachings and instructions. He tells us that discipline is a type and form of love. Oh, the Father loves us so much, he wants to take away everything that is sucking the life, sucking the energy out of me and you; some things that have clung to us and some things that we

are clinging to that just don't mean us any good. Therefore, my brothers and sisters and little ones, Jesus is telling us here that an act of love is discipline.

Now, if we refuse to accept the discipline, the pruning, the cleansing, the propping up of our God, our caretaker, there comes a time when the workmen come and take away what is dead, what is no longer productive, what is not essential for spiritual growth. That will be carried away and burned in the fire. That doesn't have to be me and that doesn't have to be you, if we just make a decision to remain in the vine. The Lord said, I'll do the work, I'll do the cultivation, I'll take care of the root system, I'll bring the sap of life up through you, I will set the bulb, I will blossom the flower, and I will bring fruit in these ways according to how you abide, how you remain. You can have a little fruit, you can have much fruit, you can have some fruit, you can have more fruit, but those of us who remain in the vine will have abundant fruit. Wouldn't you rather have abundance? Wouldn't you rather have all that God has for you?

> **You can have a little fruit, you can have much fruit, you can have some fruit, you can have more fruit, but those of us who remain in the vine will have abundant fruit.**

Then he ends on a beautiful note. After we have been lovingly disciplined, which is a type of encouragement, after we have been cultivated to grow and to thrive, he calls us friends. Oh, such love, that we are the friends of Jesus the Christ. Friendship with Jesus, fellowship divine. I'm glad to claim that Jesus is a friend of mine. I want you to look at some situations in your life where separation has been a blessing. Most of the time we consider separation as a loss where something has

been pulled away from us that we were clinging to or that might be clinging to us. But I want you to think about the times that God has allowed something to leave you and how that has blessed you.

Pastor Walter Henry Cross

Better Than New

¹ Blow a trumpet in Zion; sound an alarm on my holy mountain! Let all the inhabitants of the land tremble, for the day of the LORD is coming; it is near, ² a day of darkness and gloom, a day of clouds and thick darkness! Like blackness there is spread upon the mountains a great and powerful people; their like has never been before, nor will be again after them through the years of all generations. ³ Fire devours before them, and behind them a flame burns. The land is like the garden of Eden before them, but behind them a desolate wilderness, and nothing escapes them.

Joel 2:1-3 ESV

For this lesson we will be reading in Joel, one of the minor prophets. Now the reason that so many of those small books toward the end of the Old Testament are considered minor is because of their length, not because of content. They're just as vital and inspired as anything else within the Word of God. They are a smaller package, but they still pack a potent punch and they can help us navigate through this world here. Now, what was Joel's message? Chapter 2 opens up with a picture of devastation. We have all seen stories of devastating fires in the news. They happen everywhere and when they do, they consume property and sadly enough, lives. It can take a long time for people in regions consumed by fire to recover. Some of that recovery is mental, some is physical, some is both. Restoration is the goal and this takes strength and vitality. But there's also a time for reflection and mourning for the loss of life, loss of property, and even the loss of beautiful trees and wild flowers.

Now what is Joel referring to? He is referring to a group of people, the people of God who chose disobedience as a path of life. That's the way they were walking and that's the way they were talking. They had been warned. In fact, the chapter starts off with a warning sound, the sound of a mighty trumpet telling them that destruction is on the way. He gives a picture of devastation like a fire and nothing in the path of this fire can be saved unless the people repent, turn around, change their direction, change their heart.

Any kind of change without a heart change is no change at all.

Now, I'm not talking about going down and taking the preacher's hand, not talking about just changing your mind for a moment and changing back the next day. This is a sincere, genuine turnaround repentance. Not a repentance for show because somebody is at church with you and you want to try and impress them, not because you want a certain position within the church so you decide to go down and confess and tell people about what you have done and what your plans are for the future. The Bible describes that sort of repentance in this chapter as a renting or a tearing away, which was an emotional way of demonstrating true repentance but not changing your heart. Believe this, know this. Any kind of change without a heart change is no change at all. If you don't have Jesus Christ in your heart, then you can change your clothes, you can change what side of town you live on, you can change your name, but if your heart's not changed, you're still the same.

So, let's talk about these swarming locusts. They were aggressive. They were all-consuming. Some historians have indicated that on the day that this pestilence arose, it created a cloud so dense it could actually have blocked out the sun. It would have looked like night. Then, after the locusts were gone,

there was nothing left. All vegetation was consumed. There was nothing but pieces of straw and maybe rock there. All the trees, all the fresh vegetables, all the fruit, everything was destroyed by those swarming locusts. Well, locusts are like trouble. Talk about a swarm, sometimes trouble comes at you from all directions at the same time.

But here's the beauty part, this is where we continue the series of love. After true repentance, in that day and today, our Heavenly Father looks upon us with an eye of pity. God is so merciful and so kind and so full of grace, that after we have changed our ways, changed our mind, and changed our direction sincerely, the process of restoration begins.

Sometimes, I watch those television shows where they get an old rusty car out of the junkyard, take it to a shop, and begin restoring it. They order all-new parts, put on several coats of new paint, put on new tires, new upholstery, a new engine, new transmission, and they do it over a period of time. And, after they finished the process, the car would be new all over again. Just imagine if you had one of those '57 Chevrolets, turquoise with a white top and all that chrome, wouldn't that be beautiful? I'm old enough to remember when those cars were new and I've seen some of them in very pitiful shape. You could stick your finger through the hood if you wanted to. They've rusted out, but after restoration they were better than new.

There could be some things in your lives today that have rusted through. There could be some situations that have caused you to allow the locusts of sin to destroy all of your possibilities. But God, after repentance, will bring you back better than new. The grain came back, the fields turned green, the trees budded, and the fruit blossomed, and it was all better than it was before. God loves us so much.

I remember a time when I had to deal with a child with restorative love. First came the discipline, which we have said before is a type of love. Then after a moment of reflection, I approached my child and hugged him and let him know, Daddy

still loves you. Daddy was loving you when he was chastising you and he loves you now. You're still my wonderful son. That's what our Heavenly Father is telling us. Make sure that God's discipline doesn't create resentment in you and that your turnaround, your repentance, is genuine. Then watch God love up on you and restore the years, the life, everything that the locust has taken away. Spend a little while thinking about the process of restoration. First of all, you need to recognize what's lost. Then repent and receive the blessing of God in your life. Some of you have been through this process, some of you may be in the midst of it, so encourage each other with the true testimony of how God can make us all over again. Give thanks for the restorative love of God our Father through His Son Jesus Christ empowered by the person of the Holy Spirit.

Pastor Walter Henry Cross

My Shepherd

¹ The LORD is my shepherd; I shall not want.

⁵ You prepare a table before me in the presence of my enemies; syou anoint my head with oil; my cup overflows.

Psalm 23:1, 5

Psalm 23 is a shepherd psalm. This psalm of David deals with security and comfort. Now David was used to being isolated and being all alone away from the house, and away from his family, because of the nature of sheep. They had a certain aroma and he had to stay completely away from his home in order to be a herdsman, a shepherd. He combined his experience as a shepherd with a musical poetic setting, and we have the 23rd psalm.

One of the things that really stands out to me is that first phrase, *The Lord*. We know the Lord is over everything and if the Lord is not Lord of your life and my life, he's not Lord at all. *The Lord*. That's important to remember and to keep in front of us. He is at all times *the Lord. The Lord is my*. Now, before we get to the next word, *shepherd*, let's deal with that *my* for a minute. You know that sheep are in a herd, they're in a flock and they move about together but evidently, if you could talk to one of those little ones, they would tell you, I get personal attention from *my shepherd. My shepherd* knows my name. He calls me at the sheep gate, and I come running. He's *my shepherd*. This is very important. Now, if you take *my* off, a shepherd is just a function of employment or if you're an owner of sheep, it's just

something that you do to make money. But when you put *my* in front of it, he's actually *my* personal Shepherd. And for us to go through this world with all that's involved in it, we need to know that Jesus the Christ is our personal Shepherd.

He makes provisions. If a little sheep could talk to us, he would say, I never want for anything. There's always a table spread, there's always enough, there's always abundance, there's always green grass, not just hay and stubble and stones, there's always green grass for us to eat what we want. And if we abide with our Shepherd, if we remain and don't run off, don't run off from the congregation, don't run off from the flock, don't run off on our own, he will lead us into places of refreshment and sustenance.

And for us to go through this world with all that's involved in it, we need to know that Jesus the Christ is our personal Shepherd.

Then there is this idea about the still waters. Sheep don't like turbulence, they don't like the water when it's swirling, it scares them, makes them nervous. Well we're kind of like sheep. We don't like turbulence, we don't like frustration, we don't like aggravation, we don't like chaos. But our Shepherd comes along in the midst of all of that turbulence, and he provides a calming space for us to exist because he's our Shepherd. Let me put it this way, he's *my shepherd* and he's your Shepherd today. Sometimes, he has to make us to lie down in the green pastures because we're so busy. We're going here and yon, we're up and down and around, we're running, and we get caught up in this world. The Lord our Shepherd has to cause us to lay down, maybe not physically but to take a break, to have a stress break, a moment of reflection. It may be in the car, maybe in the shower, I don't know where but take that break that refreshes. Follow the Shepherd.

Now, what about in the presence of enemies? The banquet that's described in this psalm has to do with the animals when they are hungry and they are pressed on either side by enemies, the lion and the tiger, the bear or whatever ferocious animal might be out there in that region. The shepherd builds a wall of fire so that the sheep can eat in peace because the wild animals will see the fire and will lose their appetite for the sheep. There's a wall of protection around you, around us, when we follow our Shepherd.

Our Shepherd wants to heal us, our body, our mind, our soul, our heart, our brain, wherever we are wounded or ailing, our Shepherd wants to heal us.

The Shepherd also anoints us with oil. In James, the word anoint is used again and, in that context, it means to massage. Our Shepherd applies this medicinal, comforting, psychologically refreshing, aromatic ointment upon us. Just imagine, when you're reading your Bible, when you're singing songs to the Lord in praise and worship, when you're praying, just imagine allowing the Holy Spirit to come in and massage you, to comfort you, to be present with you. Sheep need the anointing of oil. If they don't get that anointing, flies come and lay larvae eggs in their noses and cause them to get sick. They also get scratches all over, so the shepherd anoints them very tenderly with oil and causes healing. Our Shepherd wants to heal us, our body, our mind, our soul, our heart, our brain, wherever we are wounded or ailing, our Shepherd wants to heal us.

And where is our Shepherd taking us? He's taking us to a special place. He's taking us to greener pastures. He's taking us from earth to glory. He's taking us from the mundaneness of this world to the beauty of his promise. That's the story of our

Shepherd. *My Shepherd*, he's your Shepherd, our Shepherd. I want you to think about how the Shepherd has led you. How has the Shepherd Jesus Christ led you with his crook and his staff down through the valley of the shadow of death? That valley of the shadows of death and destruction is intimidating, but look to the Shepherd. He has his lantern for light, he has his staff and his rod that protects you. He will lead you through the valley to come out on the other side.

Pastor Walter Henry Cross

How Has God Changed You?

¹ now there was a man of the pharisees named Nicodemus, a ruler of the jews. ² this man came to Jesus by night and said to him, «rabbi, we know that you are a teacher come from God, for no one can do these signs that you do unless God is with him." ³ Jesus answered him, "truly, truly, I say to you, unless one is born again he cannot see the kingdom of God."

¹⁶ "For God so loved the world, that he gave his only Son, that whoever believes in him should not perish but have eternal life.

John 3:1-3, 16 ESV

Let's go to the third chapter of John. We're going to talk about a man by the name of Nicodemus. He was a teacher of Israel so that means he was a scholar, he was a person who had studied his rabbinical studies. He had become renowned and became elevated to the position of being known as a national teacher, so he knew something. Not only was he prominent as a teacher, he was also prominent as a political and governmental official. He had a position with the Sanhedrin council, which would be equivalent to our Supreme Court. So, Nicodemus was a man of note and we see him, as the chapter opens, coming to visit Jesus by night. Interesting concept. Maybe he was busy during the day, his appointment calendar may have been full. Well, here comes Nicodemus at night, in the shadows of the evening, and that is suspect right there. Have you ever had a friend who only wanted to see you at night? Have you ever had a girlfriend, a boyfriend, some important person in your life, who only wanted to see you in the shadows?

Check that, look at that in a different light. Why do they only want to see you in the dark? I don't know about that, check that kind of love that's only available to you in the shadows of the evening.

So here comes Nick at night and like anyone who's a very prominent and intelligent and political figure, he opens up with a word of flattery. He greets Jesus by saying, Oh beloved teacher of Israel. That was fluff, that was the flattery, and Jesus cut right through it. He said, What do you want? What are you here for? Let me tell you, unless you are born again you will not be saved. Well, old Nick at night, who had been a student of various aspects of science, he realized quickly that he was in over his head and he wanted to come back at Jesus to get a point of debate and he said, How is it possible for a grown man to enter the body of his mother and be born again? And Jesus again cut through the rhetoric and said, You are a teacher of Israel, you know better. You know better than to take a metaphor for teaching and take it literally to distort the reality of what I'm saying. In other words, you know what I'm talking about, you know exactly what I'm talking about and that's the real reason you're here. You're searching, you're looking. All of your books and science and philosophy up until now have not answered all your questions. That's why you're here, Nicodemus, so let's cut to the chase. You know all of these things, yet you can't even tell me where the wind is coming from. You can't tell me where the wind is going, all you can tell me is the effect of the wind. I want to tell you about the love of God who loved us so much that he gave us an opportunity to live forever with him in harmony through Jesus Christ.

So, Nicodemus got the information, but I want you to know that something else happened that night around that fire when he met Jesus. Something that changed his life. He was old slip-and-sly Nick at night, but he became bold later on. He acknowledged Jesus in a public meeting. And then finally we see Nicodemus wrapping Jesus in a linen sheet as they

took him from the cross in the daytime. Something changed in Nicodemus. When you actually, really meet Jesus, something happens on the inside that changes you from being in the shadows of Jesus to being out front and open. Something will change you from being a secret service saint to being a person who can shout, I love Jesus from the rooftop. I believe this lesson is telling us that love makes a difference. Now if someone says they're in love with you but the mean-spiritedness, the foul language, the bitterness, does not change, that love is not making a difference in that person's life nor in your life. Don't be satisfied with a Nick at night. Be satisfied with an individual who loves you enough to own you in the daylight.

> **When you actually, really meet Jesus, something happens on the inside that changes you from being in the shadows of Jesus to being out front and open.**

Think about that beloved scripture that says *God so loved the world*. God loved the world so intensely, so completely, so divinely, that *he gave*, and you know the rest of it. Now, God has loved you so much that he gave what? We know he gave Jesus but what has God given you in your life to change you the way Nicodemus was changed? That changed you so that now you can own Jesus in the midst of controversy, in the midst of an awkward political moment, that you can own Jesus. What change did God give you?

Our Victory Dance

15 Jesus said to her, "Woman, why are you weeping? Whom are you seeking?" Supposing him to be the gardener, she said to him, "Sir, if you have carried him away, tell me where you have laid him, and I will take him away."

John 20:15 ESV

This is Resurrection Sunday morning, what a joy. He is risen, he is risen indeed. Jesus is alive, aren't you glad? I'm sitting outdoors on this beautiful, beautiful Sunday morning and I imagine when Mary went to the tomb that Sunday morning there was birds chirping in the trees, but she was sad. There was no mirth in her heart because she had lost her Savior. She was in the garden talking to herself about her sadness and her sense of loss. We read about this in the twentieth chapter of John and we're also going to look at a little bit of the first chapter of 1 Peter where we read about the victory that we have in Jesus Christ. But, back to Mary, didn't it look bad? She was sad, she was defeated, the disciples were sad, they were defeated. They were no longer around, they were scared, they were frightened, they were filled with anxiety and fear for their lives. Their leader had been executed in a very public and torturous way and now they did not know what to do next. Remember, wisdom is knowing what to do next and they didn't know. They were locked behind closed doors.

Mary and some of the other women were brave enough to prowl around the cemetery to inquire as to how Jesus was taken care of in his demise. Well, Mary looked in the tomb and she saw

two angels dressed in white — special messengers from heaven. They said to her, Why are you crying? And she said, They've taken my Savior away and we don't know where they put him, could you tell us? She went outside and there was a man standing there and she presumed that he was the gardener. He asked the same question, Why are you crying? Mary said, They've taken my Lord away. If you know where he is, we want to give him a decent burial. I'll go get him and bring him back.

Jesus is alive, he's full of power, he is a risen Savior!

Jesus is asking you this Resurrection Sunday morning, Why are you crying? Why are you defeated? Why are you so sad? Why are you so troubled? Jesus is alive, he's full of power, he is a risen Savior! He's not in stone, he's not a graven image, he's not a wooden statue. He is alive. And we have this victory and it's in Christ Jesus. *Victory in Jesus*, what a wonderful song. We don't think of it as a resurrection song, but it is. We have victory. We are no longer defeated by sin or the powers of darkness. We are no longer defeated by our habits. We're no longer defeated by people who oppose us. We're no longer defeated by conditions or circumstances or trouble in our way. We are victors, not victims. Today is a day that we can change our course and change our direction.

We are resurrection people. Now, what does that mean? That doesn't mean that we have one day a year to get some colored eggs out and celebrate Jesus being raised from the dead. We celebrate every day of the year. Every Sunday is a Resurrection Sunday at the church. That's why I'm blessed to serve. If you show up, you're going to hear about the resurrection. We need to live as though we are resurrected people. That's what Peter's talking about. We need to live as if we have the victory, as if

we're not defeated by every time the weather changes, or every time a situation changes, or every time someone else's attitude or personality changes. We are not defeated; we are resurrection people and we live in resurrection power.

The time of the Passion of Jesus Christ is a time of miracles, a time of triumphal entry, a time of a very evil atrocity done to the person and body of Jesus Christ himself but today is our victory dance. Don't stop dancing. Keep the victory alive. I want you to think about your personal victory, how you personally have been resurrected from the death of sin. Sin is death, it is separation from God. You may not cease to breathe but if you are separated from God, you're dead. Think about resurrection in your personal life from the death of sin. And if you're not there yet I want you to go get a pastor right now and talk about being resurrected.

Sweet Samples from Scripture

Pastor Walter Henry Cross

Holy Diversity

¹⁴ I am under obligation both to Greeks and to barbarians, both to the wise and to the foolish. ¹⁵ So I am eager to preach the gospel to you also who are in Rome.

Romans 1:14-15 ESV

I am so glad to announce that Jesus is alive and that he is risen indeed. What a joy we have on Resurrection Sunday morning after a weekend full of sorrow and expectation. It was sorrowful because it was our sins that took Jesus to the cross. Then we had the expectation of what was going to happen after he had been laid to rest in that borrowed tomb. Then the joy, the shouting, and the celebration on Resurrection Sunday morning as we celebrate the fact that Jesus is yet with us. This brings us to Romans the first chapter and the first 15 verses, written by Paul to the Christian believers at Rome. These individuals were living in the metropolitan area, influenced by a lot of different culture and one of the things that Paul first made clear in his writing to them is that he was a special messenger called by Jesus Christ to take the gospel of freedom to the world. First to the Jewish believers there in Rome and in other places, but also to the Greek, also to the Barbarian, also to the foreigners, also to me and you. This is an act of reconciliation. Our time together today will be spent with that word, reconciliation, which means to bring back together.

Now, you can't bring something back together if it was not together at one time. Our unity in Christ and our unity in the Lord and in the Father came at the Garden of Eden when humankind and the animal kingdom and God the Father were one. Sin developed in that context and there became a gulf fixed, a separation between God and man. We celebrated the reconciling of all that with the cross being empty on this past Sunday morning. So the question is, what are we going to do with the cross now? Is it a piece of jewelry? Is it church décor? What is it? It is a symbol of a bridge between our sin and brokenness and wholeness with the Father through Jesus Christ. What do we do with the cross more than celebrate? We're not going to wrap it up and put it up and wait for another Easter, another resurrection time. We're going to live in reconciliation love.

So the question is, what are we going to do with the cross now?

God loves us so much that he gave, we've talked about that, he gave us Jesus Christ. Not only to us, but for us to share the good news of the gospel to everybody. That's why it was so important that Paul included others when he kept reiterating to them that he had come to preach the truth. The truth of reconciliation needs to be preached to you and to your neighbor, to you and to someone who's wiser than you, to you and to someone who has not had the type of exposure you've had in terms of your education. This truth is for the wise and the foolish and you know that includes me and you, that includes us. The gospel, the good news of freedom concerning Jesus Christ, is for everybody and that is what we're talking about in terms of reconciliation love. Bringing us back through the love of God invested in His Son Jesus Christ and powered by the person of the Holy Spirit, it makes a complete circle. We're back in fellowship with the Father.

There's another word that Paul mentioned that needs to be examined in this particular context and that word is justification. Before you can come back together you've got to make some things right. When there's a breakup in the family, in relationships, you can't just show up with a dozen roses. Some of us try to do that and that just puts a Band-Aid on a very bad situation. We need to make it right. As much as lies within us, we need to make it right. We need to acknowledge the hurt, not the blame or who's at fault. We need to acknowledge that there was hurt, and that we participated in that hurt. That's not talking about right or wrong, it's talking about reality and we need to make that right. We need to say, I am indeed sorry I have offended you. You may say, But preacher, I'm not to blame. Well, we don't want to talk about who's right and who's wrong. At this point we want to talk about the restoration of relationship. That's what God did for us through Jesus Christ, he made us right. We were wrong, we know we were wrong, yes we were wrong, and we are still wrong until we accept the pardon through the blood of Jesus Christ. That resurrection moment made us right. I'm talking about Christian believers. That made us correct, that made us once again in fellowship with God the Father.

So, we see a pattern here. There needs to be some justification, that word means to be made right in our human relationships. We need to know, and we need to deal with the doctrine of justification. Then we can, through love, be reconciled back to each other. It's the same way with our Father. We need to go to the altar, it could be the altar of your heart, it could be the altar in the church, the altar in your car, the altar in your bathroom, wherever you see the need of getting right with the Lord. We need to make it right. We don't have the ability to do that within ourselves. We trust God to impute to us righteousness so we can be made right, justified in his eyesight, reconciled through the love and through the blood of Jesus Christ, and then have unity and fellowship.

Then we can experience true holy diversity. I want you to think about how we can experience reconciliation. Remember, the gospel is for the Jews, the gospel is for the Barbarian, the gospel is for the Greek, the gospel is for the foreigners, the gospel is for our neighbors, and the gospel is for me and you. How can you this day experience and be an example of true unity and diversity through the loving act of reconciliation?

How Is Jesus Your Door?

⁹ I am the door. If anyone enters by me, he will be saved and will go in and out and find pasture.

¹¹ I am the good shepherd. The good shepherd lays down his life for the sheep.

John 10:9, 11 ESV

When I think about protective love, the first thing that comes to my mind is grandparents. Those of us who've been blessed to have grandparents know that they will look out for their little bambinos. Now sometimes I'm accused of spoiling my children. If I had my grandbaby here bouncing on my knee, I wouldn't spoil him, little Walter Elijah the second, but I would guarantee you he'd end up being over-ripe. That's just what we do. We enjoy them but we also protect them. We don't want any hurt, harm, or danger to come to our own children nor to people that we love. So we get that picture of protective love.

Now, Jesus uses the metaphor of a shepherd and he really works with this idea of a gate. In some translations this would be the door or the doorway. The gate is the part of the fence that opens to let individuals in and out in ancient time. The gate of the city was the place where commerce and governmental business and community affairs took place. To go in and out of the city, you had to go through the gate. If you go in and out of an amusement park you usually have to go through a gate and you have to be checked in. In gated communities, the gate

gives residents a sense of extra protection. I'll never forget one time that I went to a community that had a gate up front, but they did not have a fence. All they had was a gate. They had come together as a community and they had this fancy gate and they had a code you put in to go in, but you could walk or drive around the gate because they did not have a fence. So, the gate was not protective, it was decorative, it gave a sense of prestige. It made a good photo op, but it didn't offer any protection.

> **A good shepherd would not go somewhere else to sleep. He would sleep at the sheep door, at the gateway, at the doorway. Therefore, Jesus called himself the doorway. He said, I am the door, I am the way. If trouble is headed your way, it has to come through me.**

Jesus talks about us as sheep and himself as the shepherd. Not only a shepherd, but a Good Shepherd, as opposed to an employee or a hireling, a person who is doing it only for the money but when trouble comes they make their exit. Jesus talked about this to the Pharisees and Sadducees. I don't know if it was on purpose or if they were just indifferent, but they didn't understand the example of Jesus being the shepherd.

Jesus told them, at night when you put your sheep up, a good shepherd would not go for a coffee break, he would not go eat his doughnuts. A good shepherd would not go somewhere else to sleep. He would sleep at the sheep door, at the gateway, at the doorway. Therefore, Jesus called himself the doorway. He said, I am the door, I am the way. If trouble is headed your way, it has to come through me. If you are going to leave, you need to leave through me, that way you have my protection.

I always suggest to young people: when you're leaving home, going into a career after high school graduation, whether it's in the world marketplace of work or into the military service or into the area of higher academics, all of those are honorable pursuits in life, all of them are good — but be careful how you leave home, how you go out of the door, how you go out of the gateway, because that gateway, even in your absence, offers you a sense of protection. God's love protects us.

Jesus is my door. Whenever you feel crowded, whenever you feel fenced in, Jesus is your door. I never felt so safe as I made my way home from school until I got inside the door. I had the protection, the warmth, the presence of family. Sometimes I encounter one of those revolving doors. I remember our utility company had one down-town and it was frightening to me because every time I'd go in the building, somehow or other I'd end up back on the sidewalk. I tried again until someone eventually pointed out to me there was another door that did not revolve. I couldn't get the timing right. I could get in but couldn't get out in time. Jesus is a protective door. He won't put you back out in the cold. He won't put you back out in danger. He will bring you into his safety, into the safety of his arms, so use that door. There are a lot of other doors that you can choose but there's only one that the Good Shepherd has for your protection.

> **There are a lot of other doors that you can choose but there's only one that the Good Shepherd has for your protection.**

I want you to think about the way in which you have protected your loved ones. Yes, you have been a door for people in your life. Sometimes knowingly, sometimes unknowingly. Sometimes you've been that invisible person who stood and watched over a child while they were playing. They didn't know you were there,

but you were their escape door. Sometimes you were their fire escape when life began to billow up around them. Sometimes you're their door of opportunity, while you are training and developing them to be all that they can be. Think about those opportunities you've had in life and then go over to the spiritual core of it. How has Jesus been that door for you? That door of opportunity? That door of escape? That door of provision? Jesus is the door, he's the way, he's the light.

Jonah

Sweet Samples from Scripture

Pastor Walter Henry Cross

Your Jonah Moment

¹⁷ And the LORD appointed a great fish to swallow up Jonah. And Jonah was in the belly of the fish three days and three nights. ...

¹ Then Jonah prayed to the LORD his God from the belly of the fish, ...

¹⁰ And the LORD spoke to the fish, and it vomited Jonah out upon the dry land.

Jonah 1:17, 2:1, 10 ESV

We have been examining the love of Jesus as a shepherd, his protective love, his providing love, his prevailing love, and the love that has been over us like a warm blanket. Now we're continuing that love theme but with a new character, Jonah. Jonah's father's name meant truth and that indicates to us that Jonah was brought up in a household where truth was prevailing. He was aware of what truth was and what falseness would be. In addition to that, we later find out that Jonah received a call from God. So, two things we know about Jonah are that he was brought up in a house where truth was important and, later on, he was aware of the voice and call of God.

As a prophet, Jonah received an assignment to go to Nineveh to speak on behalf of God. Nineveh was a great city of the Assyrians, who were a natural enemy of the people of God. Therefore, Jonah did not want to go. He was reluctant, rebellious. He began to think in his mind whether he should go or not, and finally he came to the point where he refused to go. Now God had a different opinion. When God tells us to do

something, that's really what he wants us to do. Let's see how God's love interceded.

Jonah did go, but he went in the wrong direction. He went toward Tarsus, not toward Nineveh. He didn't get confused on his road map, he didn't input the wrong thing on his GPS, his GPS didn't malfunction. Remember, he's been rebellious and reluctant and refusing and now he's running. He's running away from God. Many of us know that when you run away from God — I don't care what kind of Nikes or tennis shoes you've got on — you're not going to get very far.

I want you to be aware of this: every step away from God is down. Anytime we make a decision to delay, to defer, to rebel, to be reluctant, to refuse, our steps away from God are downward.

So, Jonah goes through this series of down-ness. He went down from Jerusalem, he went down to the seashore, he went down in the boat, he went down in the water, he went down in the fish's belly. Notice I didn't say whale. The Bible said that God prepared a big fish. The whale story sounds cute but it's probably not accurate. God prepared a big fish, just custom-built for Jonah and his rebelliousness. The people on the boat noticed that something was going wrong. They were not followers of Yahweh, but they were religious people. They had their own idols and they said to Jonah, Man your God's mad with you and if you stay on board, you're going to mess us all up. So, over the side of the boat he goes. Again, headed downward, down into the water, then down into the fish's belly.

I want you to be aware of this: every step away from God is down. Anytime we make a decision to delay, to defer, to rebel, to

be reluctant, to refuse, our steps away from God are downward. Now the fish that God designed just for Jonah got sick and tired of Jonah's sinful self and redeposited him on the shore. After that trip in the fish's belly, Jonah changed his mind. He had a repentant moment. He changed his mind, changed his attitude, changed his thinking; he moved toward Nineveh in a most expeditious manner and did the will of God.

I want you to think about how you have refused, rebelled, been reluctant, or have run away from God when God was calling you. Think about the consequences of disobedience and the consequences of refusing to do the will of God. Now, maybe some of you are in that Jonah mode right now. You've got one foot over the side of the boat and you are going down. Not necessarily for the last count because God's loving mercy is there as a life preserver, but if you keep going down, guess where you're going to end up? Out of fellowship with God, and I know you don't want that. So think about how your Jonah moment in your life has gone, how God has rescued you by his love and established you and then headed you to the place where he wants you to go.

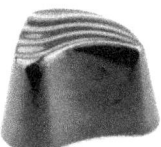

God Is a Keeper

¹ Then Jonah prayed to the LORD his God from the belly of the fish, ² saying, «I called out to the LORD, out of my distress, and he answered me; out of the belly of Sheol I cried, and you heard my voice.

Jonah 2:1-2 ESV

Jonah walked away from God. As he went down from Jerusalem and down to the seashore and down into the bottom of the boat, he encountered a great storm. When we walk away from God, a lot of times we are headed right toward a storm. Jonah sailed away. He sailed away from God's will, from God's word, and God's way, and he encountered opposition in the elements that pushed against him. The men on the boat made a decision, a choice that was permitted by God, to cast him overboard. Jonah realized that he was the hindrance, he was the one on board that was causing all the confusion, and so he decided to permit this unceremonial exit from the boat.

Now, we find out, as we look in the second chapter of Jonah, that Jonah was having a prayer meeting with God. He realized the error of his ways, he realized the fact that he had walked away from God and had encountered an problem for himself and had caused problems for other people. When we do not do the will of God, we only bring trauma to ourselves and others. So, that's what was going on. He went over the side of the ship and he prayed to God: Lord, I got myself in a terrible fix, will you help me? Now, like David, before the end of Jonah's crisis he began a series of praise: Lord I thank you, I thank

you that you know where I am, that you know I'm walking in disobedience, that you know I'm not where I should be. I should be on my way to a place where you've called me to preach but I chose to go to a place where I can play.

Here we see a very key element in the story of Jonah. He began to praise and thank the Lord prior to his deliverance because he knew something about the Lord. He knew that the Lord is a keeper. The Lord is one who preserves us, who keeps us, who takes care of us when we don't have the ability to take care of ourselves. Splish-splash, Jonah's in the middle of the ocean and he describes this. He says that he was wrapped up in seaweed, he was going down for the last count, he couldn't even free his arms, his head was covered with debris. He began to go down and down and down and down. Every step away from God is down.

> **The Lord is one who preserves us, who keeps us, who takes care of us when we don't have the ability to take care of ourselves.**

Suddenly a prepared fish saw a tasty morsel and swallowed him whole. In this new environment he continued his plea to the Lord for deliverance. He felt that he had received his just rewards, he felt that he had been disobedient and the God he served was a righteous God and was giving him right what he deserved. That was justice and a lot of times we're walking in justice as we get the results of our own mess-ups. But don't you know, God can bless our mess? Here's Jonah — he's in a heck of a fix. He's in a big mess down there with all those gastric juices inside that prepared animal of marine life. He probably couldn't see too much because it was dark, but he could smell what was going on and it was horrible. He described the whole situation of walking away from God as just like being in hell. He'd never been there before but I guarantee you this was close enough.

All of a sudden, this sinful individual made the creation of God sick to his stomach and when Jonah thought he was going down for the last time, when he felt it was lights out for him, when he thought it was all over and he was going to die in his sins, this fish coughed him up on the shore. Oh, the Lord's a keeper. The Lord has kept us. He has kept me, and he has kept you despite ourselves. In the midst of our wickedness, he has kept us. That night we went the wrong way at the wrong speed to see the wrong person to do the wrong thing, he kept us. That day when we said the wrong thing to the wrong person and thought we got away with it, the Lord kept us. That moment we thought the wrong thought and invented the wrong plan and thought we were smarter than the average person, God kept us. God is a keeper. He preserves us.

We like to refer to it as grace, but the grace was with Jonah all the while when he went down to the fish's stomach and when he came up and got back on solid ground. Where have you been where you shouldn't have? What have you done that you shouldn't have? What have you said that you shouldn't have, and the Lord kept you? Somebody didn't pull out a pistol or a razor and rearrange your face, or the elements, the wind, the storms of life did not consume you, or the prepared fish that stopped you in your tracks did not give you what you really deserved. Separation from God is death, but God kept you. What are some of the various ways that God has kept you in life up into this very moment? How can you encourage someone else to know that God is a keeper? Be glad he kept you, I'm glad he kept me.

Sweet Samples from Scripture

Pastor Walter Henry Cross

Your *Then* Moment

¹ Then the word of the LORD came to Jonah the second time, saying, ² "Arise, go to Nineveh, that great city, and call out against it the message that I tell you." ³ So Jonah arose and went to Nineveh, according to the word of the LORD. Now Nineveh was an exceedingly great city, three days' journey in breadth.

Jonah 3:1-3 ESV

Remember Jonah? Jonah was the one who went down from Jerusalem, went down to the seashore, went down in the boat, went down in the water, and went down in the fish's belly. Then he was deposited back up on the shoreline. The Word of God says that he began to run toward his previously assigned destination, the great city of Nineveh. This city was so big it would take a man probably three days to walk across it. That's a pretty good-sized city and when Jonah arrived there, I can imagine that he looked a little different after spending all that time in the water and spending all that time in the fish. He probably looked fierce; maybe his skin was bleached and spotty, and his clothes looked rough, but he had the word from the Lord. That's important for us to remember. When God gives you an assignment, it's not about what you look like, it's about obedience and doing the will of God and following his way.

Now, when Jonah chapter 3 opens, something very important happens. It says *then*. There's a *then* in all of our lives. After all of that reluctance, after all of that rebellion, after all of that regret, God puts a *then* right there in the beginning of

chapter 3. Then Jonah received instruction from God for the second time. That's very significant. Is there a second time in your life? I know there's more than two, three, four in mine, when God readdresses an issue. God says, You have been rebellious but you repented, you have been reluctant but you decided to go, and now I'm calling you again. Oh, be so overjoyed if the Lord ever calls you a second time. That's such a privilege.

Again the Lord calls Jonah and gives him the same assignment: go to that great city and tell them. Now, what was the message? The message was this: in forty days, if you don't straighten up and fly right, you're going to live crooked and die wrong. I've already stationed some individuals to come and eat your lunch and clean your plate. Danger is impending at the door because of your disobedience. The king of the city heard the message and the king and his leadership participated in repentance. That's important, people. The leadership participated in the repentance and getting right with God. That's an individual thing so we see that the men and the women, the boys and the girls, the families all went on a fast. Even the animals were on a fast.

Oh, be so overjoyed if the Lord ever calls you a second time. That's such a privilege.

Why would the animals have to be sanctified unto the Lord? The reason was God wanted the people to spend time with him and feeding the cattle would have taken time away from the Lord. Feeding yourself sometimes takes time away from the Lord. You'd be surprised how many people show up at Sunday school late because of Bojangles and McDonald's. A fast is not a diet program, a fast is more than just not eating, it's when you consecrate your time unto the Lord. Read up on it, don't go

and do anything because you saw it on television or you went to a conference and saw forty-days this, that, and the other. Read, study, pray about it. Those of you who may be on special medications, talk to your doctor about it. Find out what's the difference between a denial and a fast.

The people were serious about their repentance and they stopped eating long enough to hear from the Lord. They stopped doing their chores long enough to hear from the Lord. We don't see where any of the animals died but we do see where they were saved. So, Jonah preached the Word of God. He finally did what the Lord asked him to do. Now, my brothers and sisters, is there a *then* in your life? After you've repented, after you have shaken your finger symbolically or literally in the face of the Lord and told the Lord what you were not going to do, after you left that church, left that position, left that relationship, left that job, and looked back and said I don't care, has God called you again? Repentance renews our relationship with the Lord. God called Jonah again and he was obedient. He ran toward the assignment God gave him, he was anxious, he had a renewed spirit, he had a touch of revival. The Lord is calling you, he's calling me, he's calling for the second, third, and fourth time. What are we going to say? Let today be your *then* moment, your epiphany, that moment in time when you realize that your arms are too short to fight with God. This may be the very moment when you hear God calling you a second time.

Sweet Samples from Scripture

Pastor Walter Henry Cross

Watch Out for the Jonah Spirit

¹ But it displeased Jonah exceedingly, and he was angry. ² And he prayed to the LORD and said, "O LORD, is not this what I said when I was yet in my country? That is why I made haste to flee to Tarshish; for I knew that you are a gracious God and merciful, slow to anger and abounding in steadfast love, and relenting from disaster. ³ Therefore now, O LORD, please take my life from me, for it is better for me to die than to live."
⁴ And the LORD said, "Do you do well to be angry?"

Jonah 4:1-4 ESV

Jonah was the reluctant prophet who wanted to do anything but the will of God, but he got his act together and he ended up going where God told him to go which was the great city of Nineveh. After his experience in the deep, he decided to become a compliant prophet and go and do the will of God. When he went to the great city, he began to preach and teach what God had told him which was a very serious warning to the people to get their act together because God had made a decision to deal with them in a strong and powerful way if they remained in their state of disobedience. The people of Ninevah heard Jonah and there was a great revival. They went on a fast, they sanctified themselves, consecrated their animals, and even the leadership got involved. In our churches and systems and organizations, if our leadership is not on board, a whole lot doesn't take place, doesn't happen, just doesn't get done. It starts with leaders. So, teachers, pastors, individuals, board chairmen, if you're in a leadership position, be like the

king of Nineveh who went with the people into repentance. Be a leader in every situation.

Don't you think that Jonah would have been happy that the people turned to God? Don't you think that Jonah would've been overjoyed that his message had such an effect that the people decided to do away with their evil ways and do away with their idolatry and follow the Lord Jehovah, Yahweh? Well, that's not how the story ends. Jonah gets upset with God. We know he gets upset with God because he declares, I knew you were that type of God, I knew you were loving, I knew you were kind, I knew you were patient, I knew you were forgiving, I knew you would not allow the people to suffer the sentence of death you had prescribed for them if they turned from their evil ways.

So, we gather that part of Jonah's reluctance was that he did not want the people to be saved. Why? There were some historical reasons. Jonah believed that the people of Nineveh were some of *those people*, people who didn't deserve to be saved. Have you ever been one of *those people* in someone else's life? Have you ever accused someone of being one of *those people*? Sometimes we do it very subtly, we have a low expectation of *those people*. We'll say, Don't you know how *those people* act? Don't you know how *those people* do? We say it even though we have been on the other end of being accused of being *those people*, people who live on that side of town or who have a certain behavior. These Ninevites had been the enemies of the people of God back in Jerusalem and Jonah had not forgotten every evil word that had been spoken, every evil deed that had been committed, every battle, every death, every act of bullying. He kept all this close to his heart and when God saved the people, Jonah said, I can't stand this. I can't stand it, *those people* are too evil to be saved, and God, I blame you for it.

Then he went into pout mode. Now, this is an indication of immaturity. He went into pout mode, his poked his lip out, and went up on the side of the hill. When the Lord showed him how the people were responding well to the will of God, Jonah

got his backpack and took his blanket out. He traveled with a blanket for shelter and he probably hung it up on a rock or something. He made up a covering for himself and he sat there, and he decided to be suicidal. In other words, he said, If I can't have my way, God just take me out. If I can't have my way in the choir, I just won't sing. If I can't have my way as the chairman of this board, I'll quit. If I can't have my way as the head of this organization, you just find somebody else. Have you ever heard that before? That's a Jonah spirit. If I can't have it my way, I won't participate. Lord, just take me on out. Maybe they'll find somebody else, maybe they'll find someone better me. That's when we try to sound noble, but really what we're saying is, Lord, if I can't have my way — I don't want your way, I want my way — if I can't have my way, I don't want to have any part of it.

Well, the Lord sent a protective bush to grow up over Jonah to give him shade from the deathly wind of heat in the desert. The Lord still loved Jonah. Jonah had run away before, and now he's running again. This time, he's running from the truth. He's running from the truth that God loves everybody. He doesn't want to deal with that because Jonah doesn't love everybody. So, here comes this bush, it gives him shade, lowers the temperature, gives him comfort. He gets a good nap and relaxes. Then God takes the bush away and Jonah complains. The Lord says, Why are you mad? Has the Lord ever asked you that? Why are you upset? I was the one who died for you, now why are you mad? Where are the nail scars in your hand? Where is the wound in your side? And you have the nerve to be mad?

Well, Jonah was just like that, just like the way we act sometimes, immature, mad. Maybe Jonah said, When you gave me the bush, I was glad about that. And the Lord said, But why are you mad now? Because you took it back, says Jonah. Well, everything is for a reason and for a season. The Lord tells Jonah, I love the people of Nineveh and they have been saved, and you can't get happy over that. You didn't plant the bush,

the bush is not yours, and when I took the bush back, you got mad over the bush. You can't celebrate the power of salvation for the people of Nineveh, but you mourn over a bush that you did not plant and that did not belong to you.

And that's where the story ends, but we need to consider something. We need to consider Jonah's attitude. A lot of times we ask, Why did the Lord end the story there? Because he told us everything in the body of that prophecy that we need to know for our lives today. You can make some theological notions as to what happened to Jonah, whether he got saved or what might have happened to him. God gave us what is important. What is important is for us to think about where we are sitting. Are we hidden under a bush? Are we hoping that the Lord gives somebody what we think they have coming to them? How many times have you said, I hope she gets what she's got coming to her?

Then we like to talk about the theology of reciprocity. We always like to get into whatever you sow, you're going to reap. I'm going to tell you a secret: if you and I reaped what we'd sown, we wouldn't be sitting here today. Watch out for that Jonah spirit. Be thankful when the Lord saves somebody, because he saved me and you. That Jonah spirit crops up in all of our lives. What can we do about it? How can we repent of it? How can we avoid it? How can we love everybody? If they are a different religion, a different race, if they live on a different side of town, how can we embrace and love everybody and avoid the spirit of Jonah?

Pastor Walter Henry Cross

God with Us

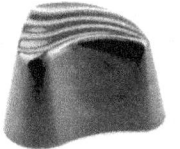

Pastor Walter Henry Cross

Again and Again

¹ After Ehud's death, the Israelites again did evil in the LORD's sight. ² So the LORD turned them over to King Jabin of Hazor, a Canaanite king. The commander of his army was Sisera, who lived in Harosheth-haggoyim. ³ Sisera, who had 900 iron chariots, ruthlessly oppressed the Israelites for twenty years. Then the people of Israel cried out to the LORD for help.

Judges 4:1-3

God has an enormous capacity for love. And God wants us to follow his example and increase our capacity to love. Now let's go into another area of the first dispensation in the Old Testament, to the first group of teachings and doctrines that we have, and and look at the fascinating story about Deborah and Barak. This was the time of the judges; they were men and women who are assigned by God to judicate what was going on in the lives of his people at that time. Deborah is well known because of her heroism and because of the fact that she heard the will of God and did it. The story starts off in Judges 4 with something that tells us a lot about the capacity of the love of God and also about the people of God at that time. It says, *again* Israel has strayed from the teachings of Almighty God. They have gone a-whoring after other nations. They made choices to go with the trend instead of the divine. They were dealing with what came naturally to them, which is sin — what comes naturally to us is sin — that's the path that's popular, that's the path that's trendy, that's glitzy, and that's the path that they often found themselves in. Here's the cycle: sin, captivity, punishment,

deliverance, restoration. Sin, which is disobedience, captivity, punishment, deliverance, restoration.

The Lord had a plan for Israel, but they had their own plan. They had their own idea. They wanted to go their own way and it only caused them deep pain and heartache. Today, my brothers and sisters, and boys and girls, if you follow your plan, if it's not ordained of God, you're going to find yourself involved in sin, you're going to be captivated by sin and it's going to take you away from all the places that you want to be. Then through repentance and prayer, deliverance will come. After deliverance, we have a choice: we can return to our old way of doing things or we can live for God.

The story goes that while Deborah was away from her palm trees, her palm grove where she would meet with the people and discuss the needs that they had, there was an occasion where the Lord spoke to her and said, I want to deliver the people of God. Let me tell you what was going on. Around the people of God were all these nations that were oppressing them. They were warlike people, they were strong in mighty numbers, and there had been unrest in the land for 20 years. So, the Lord told Deborah, If you will go into battle, I will go ahead of you, ahead of the army, and with you; my angels will deliver the enemy into your hand. Deborah, full of excitement, tasting victory, called one of the military generals, Barak, and said to him, Did you hear the Lord saying let's go to war? Not only did God call her, not only was she certain of the calling, she was certain of the commandment. She had a divine strategic plan. A lot of times we fail because we don't wait on the plan. We hear part of what God says, but we don't hear all of what God is saying. But Deborah heard exactly what the Lord said, and the Lord said, Let's go.

Well, Barak was somewhat troubled by this revelation. I don't know if he had heard it before Deborah or maybe this was the first time. I know in the scripture it says that Deborah said to him, Didn't you hear? Get up and go. Barak said, Alright, but

I've got a proposition for you: I'll go if you go with me. Now, I don't know what his train of thought was. Did he think that she was weak because she was a woman and that she wouldn't go, so that would give him an excuse not to go? Did he think that the nation would be humiliated on the field of battle and he was wiser than her because he had been in many battles and maybe she hadn't? I don't know what his train of thought was. There's a whole lot of speculation and some of you scholars may have more information about that than I know. But I know this; she said, Let's go. She did not hesitate because she had faith in God. She was sure of God's calling. She was sure of God's commandment. She was sure of victory.

They went to the mountain that God told her to go to, and they camped out on the mountain. Now, one of the reasons that our brother was so frightened was because of modern weaponry technology. The opposing army had ten thousand ironclad chariots. This army, powerfully equipped with metal, could annihilate anybody in any other skirmish that they got involved in on the field of battle. They probably had been doing just that for the last twenty years. But the plan was to go up on the mountain, call them to battle and, when they assembled, swoop down upon them. Now, if you read the scripture real close, you'll find that some of the lieutenants in the battle were equipped with sticks. We've got iron chariots on the enemy side, and we've got sticks on the Lord's side. Guess who won. The Lord gave them the victory of the day.

When we go to chapter 5, we see another interesting story taking place. Here, Deborah is singing her war song of victory. She tells the story of how God gave her the plan, how the plan was implemented, and how the victory was won. She talks about how Barak got the courage not only to lead the troops into battle with her by his side, but also to chase after this foreign king and send him running all the way down to a tent where Jael lived. In the song, Jael had already killed the king, taking a tent peg and driving it through his

head. This is how it happened. The king showed up, he was running for his life, and he said, the enemy is behind me, will you take me in? Jael said, Sho'nuff. She took him in, and he said, I'm thirsty, I've been running hard, can I have some water? She said, No, no, let's give you some buttermilk. Yes, it's in the Bible, buttermilk mixed with honey. It was sweet, it was soothing, it was comforting. You can't have fresh milk in the desert, so it had turned what we would call sour. They sweetened it up with honey, so it wasn't the type of milk that would make him sick or poisoned, but it was the type of milk that gave him the most peaceful rest he ever had. Jael talked real calm to him, he went to sleep and, as they used to say back in the country where I come from, he woke up dead. We know there's no such thing, it's just a saying, but he closed his eyes never to raise them up again. And even in Deborah's song, the king's mother was waiting for him to come and by the length of the time that passed she kind of realized that her son was not coming back home.

So, there are some interesting things in this lesson. One is about leadership. People will follow you if you're excited about where you're going. Deborah was excited about going to Mount Tabor. She was excited and the army was energized by her excitement, her confidence in the Lord. Also, she did something else that's very interesting. I don't know whether me and you would do it or not, but she gave Barak credit. We know he was a little weak in the knees, we know he hesitated, he paused, he thought long and hard, he made an ultimatum that he would go only if she went with him. But when Deborah sang her song, she talked about how the Lord had blessed her and Barak. Did he deserve the credit? But here's the main thing: God's capacity to love his people. He keeps on loving us when we sin and get captivated and taken away by our own devices. He allows us the blessed privilege of repenting and then he restores and delivers us.

Pastor Walter Henry Cross

Can God Use Your Weakness?

¹⁵ "But Lord," Gideon replied, "how can I rescue Israel? My clan is the weakest in the whole tribe of Manasseh, and I am the least in my entire family!" ¹⁶ The LORD said to him, "I will be with you. And you will destroy the Midianites as if you were fighting against one man."

Judges 6:15-16 TLB

In Judges, chapters 6 through 8, we read the story of Gideon. Gideon was a judge and he became a very strong leader in Israel. But it didn't start off that way. When our story begins, we find a recurring pattern. The pattern is that Israel has sinned and is in the process of being punished. They are on their way to repentance and then deliverance and restoration. They have become involved again in idol worship with foreign gods. God has instructed them well as to what they were supposed to do, but they have chosen their own path and they are being indifferent to the instructions of the Lord. This story tells us more about the character of God, his patience, his forbearance, his love, and His mercy.

As the scene opens, we see Gideon. His name means that he's a forester, he's a worker with wood, he cuts down trees. Kind of like Jesus, whose earthly occupation was carpentry, Gideon was a type of woodworker out in the forest, cutting and falling trees. His village is under siege. The Midianites would often come to the area and plunder them. They would go into the garden and the farmland and get all of the food, and would take away all of the farm animals. They would wait until it was harvest time and come and eat their lunch, literally take their food. They

would use starvation as a weapon or as a tactic to submit them to their authority. As a result, the men and women and the families of Gideon's village would go up into the mountains. They would dig places for shelter and cover them with debris and brush in order to survive this onslaught of the enemy. They had to hide their food.

So, we see Gideon down in a winepress preparing wheat, hiding wheat. It's interesting that he's in a wine press, a place where they would keep crushed grapes and make grape juice and wine. Also, since bread is made from wheat, there may be some type of correlation between bread and wine and that being the place where Lord finds him. Here comes an angel of the Lord and he says, O mighty, valiant man. Gideon sort of says, That title doesn't fit me. And Gideon says, very respectfully, Almighty God, where have you been? Don't you know that for about seven years we've been catching it down here? You brought us out of Egypt, how come you can't get us out of this? Now, Gideon's just like me and you; when things go wrong, we have a tendency to blame God. What went wrong? Sin. What's the result of sin? Distance from God. But God shows up in the middle of their punishment to give a prophetic voice: I am still with you.

Gideon, like so many other mighty leaders in the Bible, first resisted. Moses said he couldn't talk and Barak said he could go but he needed someone else to go with him. Gideon's just like me and you when that call comes upon our lives, and everybody that's reading this has a call on their lives. Just like us, we offer an excuse; that's not for me, I'm not able, I'm not equipped, I'm not educated, I can't afford it, I've got something else I've got to do, Lord you know where I am, you know what's going on in my life, they won't listen to me. We're in a hole in the ground just like Gideon, we're in that vat of grapes or that container of wheat and we are not hearing what God has to say. Now, how did God resolve this? He told Gideon, I'll go with you. If there's a call of God on your life, and there is, God will go with you.

Gideon said, I'm from the poorest tribe, the poorest community, the poorest family. I've got all these dead brothers, it's just me and daddy, and I'm the youngest and the weakest and the most coward one of the whole group. How can you use me? God said, I'll go with you. So the Lord gives him an assignment. Tear down your household idol. You've got to clean up at home if you're going to be a good leader. Tear down your household idol. Cut it down, destroy it, burn it up. Well, that was going against culture, that was going against the grain. Gideon was so upset and so frightened by this assignment that he did it at night. He got ten men together and he cut down this tower at night, this idol, this pole. The next morning, the community was in an uproar. They asked Gideon's daddy, what did your little boy do? He's going to make the gods mad with us. His dad was very wise. He said, Well, you don't have to take up for the god. If he's a real god, he'll take up for himself.

What's the result of sin? Distance from God. But God shows up in the middle of their punishment to give a prophetic voice: I am still with you.

That was the launching point where we see Gideon going to do the will of God. Now, he had some other little spots of hesitation, you know the story well about the fleece, this little woolen piece of cloth he put out and found wet, and then he put out and found dry. God tolerated him and he tolerates us in our disbelief, in our hesitancy, in our reluctance. Well, Gideon got through all of that and then God allowed him to gather the troops together because it was time for this contest of the warriors. And God said, I think you're still scared. Gideon said, Uh-huh. So, God said, I want you to do something. Get somebody with you and go down as a spy. Gideon said, Me, go down as a spy? You know they don't like me. But God said, You go down there and I'll go with you. I just want you to go

down there this night to the camp. So, Gideon went down to the camp and he overheard two of the Midianites talking. One of them said, I had a dream last night that a barley loaf of bread came rolling out of the hills, devoured our campsite, and took over the whole troop of army down here. And the other one said, you know what that means? No, said the first one, tell me what it means. It means that Gideon, a mighty man of God, is going to take his sword and come down and devour us. You see, the enemy had a better concept of who Gideon was than Gideon himself. The enemy is more afraid of us than we have knowledge of ourselves. We are more powerful in the eyes of the enemy than we are in our own mirror.

You know the story about how the final selection was made. They started with many, many thousands of troops and the Lord told Gideon to tell all the ones who were scared to go home, and they did. They said, Well, we heard that, we won't wait around. We'll pray for you, but we're gone, we're out of here. Gideon used other methods of selection and got down to 300 men. Now, in my heritage, a lot of preaching is made out of how they lapped water like a dog or took the time to bowl the water in the hands. Some have said that what you have to do is drink water and keep your hand on your sword at the same time. Different things have been made of this and there's a lot of good preaching. This was God's method of selection for this particular situation and you can put a lot into it, but the main point is that God did it. God can take over a powerful enemy with a few people who are listening to the Lord.

The Lord said, Take your meager army and surround these thousands of Midianites. Take a torch, take a clay pitcher, and take a horn. Now, what kind of weaponry is that? God said it, I believe it, I'm going to do it. God said it, and whether I believe it or not, God still can do it. So, they surround the enemy, they follow the Lord's instructions, they smash those clay pots in the middle of the night and it sounds to the Midianites like thousands of people are on the surrounding mountains getting ready to swoop

down on them. Then Gideon's army lights all the torches, and the Midianites see all the woods that night just light up bright all around them. They hear the horns blow, and they don't know what it is, but it's loud. They hear all of this and they get scared. They get up and go to running, and they start fighting themselves, they draw their swords on each other, and the bravery returns to Gideon. He chases them down and he wins the day.

God can take over a powerful enemy with a few people who are listening to the Lord.

Now Gideon had some trouble back home. The elders of the city still weren't quite too sure about him. On his way to the battle, you remember, he stopped and asked for some refreshments for the troops. They said, Well, we don't know, you go win the battle, then we'll think about it. He went back to those same elders of the city and he had to deal with them and tell them the truth. He had to tell them, the Lord has given me the battle.

The people of God then had forty years of peace. The point of our story today is that God can do it, in spite of us. He has chosen to use us. God can use the weakest, the person with the least resources How can I testify to that? Because he used me and still is using me, and I'm grateful this morning. I want you to think about how God can use your weakness to win his battle.

Sweet Samples from Scripture

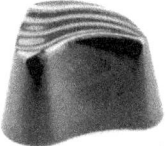

Keeping Your Word to God

³⁰ And Jephthah made a vow to the LORD. He said, "If you give me victory over the Ammonites, ³¹ I will give to the LORD whatever comes out of my house to meet me when I return in triumph. I will sacrifice it as a burnt offering."

Judges 11:30-31

Jephthah, a judge in Israel, had a very interesting beginning to life. His father gave him his beginning by having what we might call an affair or a relationship with someone that was not his wife. Jephthah was born of a prostitute, according to the Bible. Now, before you beat up on his dad, that was a socially acceptable behavior at that time, though not so much today. When Jephthath became a certain age, his brothers decided that he did not need to belong to the family any longer. They hadn't had a shock of morality; they were just interested in the bottom line figure. To them, Jephthath was someone that they could eliminate from the family so that the inheritance from their father would be greater among them. So, they did not desire him to be their brother any longer. They got together, they organized in strength and they expelled him from the family.

He went up to another area and he associated himself with some individuals that were probably known bandits and thieves and robbers. He almost instantly became their leader. He had leadership in him and we're learning something about how God operates and judges. He picks individuals that are the most unlikely to succeed according to the eye and the filter of

men and women. There's somebody that you know who never thought you'd be sitting where you are today. They had another plan for you, they had a different expectation, but the Lord blessed you and look at where you are now.

So, Jephthah was one of those individuals who had a difficult start to life. He was expelled by what he thought were his own brothers, he may have not known any different. He went up and had to live and learn on the street how to survive. Now, in due process of time, and you'll find this very often in the Bible, you'll find it very often in life, the people who have kicked up their heels against you need you now. So, there was an attack on the region where Jephthah was living. They sent a dispatch to him and they said, We need you, we need your army, we need your men. This is the same man that they had expelled, the same one that they had looked down on, the same one that they didn't want to split the inheritance with. Jephthah asked the same question that me and you would ask. Why do you need me now? What's going on there? Now that you're desperate, you're speaking and singing a different tune.

Let's look at the character of Jephthah. He was a leader. He had his own troop. They had been ridiculed as being the baser sorts of life. But when his hometown, his brothers and his sisters were in jeopardy, he did not take it out against them. He swallowed his pride, went back, and led them to victory. It was a tremendous victory.

Not only was he a person of great valor, and great strength, and had organizational skills, but according to the Bible, he also had a sense of diplomacy. One of the individuals that had just been raising all kind of havoc against the people of God asked Jephthah a question when they came to have a diplomatic meeting. This individual, who was the enemy at that time, said to him, We want our land back. Jephthah was diplomatic, he was shrewd, he was a street person. He said, Well, let me tell you, look at history. God gave us the land. Your facts are misconstrued. God asked us to leave Egypt and go

to the promised land and when we had to come through your territory, you and some other nations decided to barricade us, to interrupt our flow, and we had to go miles and miles around. God gave us this land because of your historical stubbornness and your unwillingness to provide us safe passage through.

You see, the people had heard what happened in Egypt, and about what happened to the Pharaoh. They had heard about the ten plagues, and about how the Egyptians almost paid them to leave. They had heard how the Israelites had grown from 70 people to thousands and thousands of people and they were frightened. They were afraid that if they allowed the Israelites to come through, they would take over the land. They presumed that the Israelites were a warlike people. They were actually a peace-loving people, but they would fight if God directed them to. Now, years later, Jephthah knew his history. He knew the history of his people. That's important, scholars. We need to share our history, our local church history, our heritage as a people, our heritage as Christians, our heritage as a nation. The young ones who are down in the cradle right now need to start knowing our history.

Well, Jephthah made a decision. He said, Lord, if you give me this battle, whoever comes out of my house when I get back, I will sacrifice them to you. He made a vow to the Lord. So, he went into battle and the Lord did what the Lord always does, he gave Jephthah the victory of the day. Jephthah marched back home and guess who came out of his house first? It was his own daughter. Now this was problematic, this was sad, this is the part of story that I always wish had a different ending, but it doesn't. He had said whoever comes out of the house, he would sacrifice to the Lord. His daughter, who came out playing her tambourines and dancing and being glad that her daddy was back, noticed that dad wasn't happy. She said, What's the matter, dad? And he said, I have opened my mouth to the Lord. I told him whoever comes out of the house first I would give in a sacrifice of burnt offering.

Notice her response. Dad, you have said it and I want you to carry through with what you promised the Lord. What character, she must have learned it from her dad and/or mom. She had deep character. Whatever you promised the Lord, you need to do it. Some of us don't fear the Lord enough today to make a promise and keep it. We say stuff like, Lord, if you save me from this situation, from this circumstance, from this disease, from this opportunity, or condition, Lord, if you save me from all of this, I will follow you. Then we'll show up at church that first Sunday. We'll sit there and smile and thank the Lord, we might even testify. But three months later, we can't be found. That's so sad.

But Jephthah kept his vow. I don't know what he actually did. I know that the Bible says that he kept his vow. His daughter said, Give me a reprieve, let me go up into the mountains for two months and after I grieve my virginity, I'll show back up. And she showed back up just like she said she would. She kept her vow just like he kept his vow and he did as unto the Lord what he had promised. Now, notice that God did not demand that sacrifice. God did not ask him to give up his daughter. God did not tell him to make that vow. It was an unwise vow. Quit negotiating with God. We don't have anything that God needs, so don't negotiate with God. Just say yes.

Well, did he kill her? According to the Bible, it kind of looks like it. There's some other theories if you want to study them. If you want to go deep into the languages, there's a possibility that he gave her away for religious service, like being a nun. Remember, when she was in the mountains, she mourned not for her life but for her virginity, so she may have become a temple worker and stayed in the temple for the rest of her life, unmarried. That might have been part of the offering, we don't know, that's speculation. We don't know exactly, but we know this: he kept his vow. Maybe he was expecting a servant, we don't know who or what he was expecting. God never gave him the right to just ruthlessly — he was not at war anymore

— kill someone in his household or staff or his family. That's a position he took upon himself.

So be careful what you promise the Lord because whatever you promise the Lord, you owe. Think about the character of Jephthah. He was ostracized by his own brothers, but he came back to save them. He promised his own daughter and he followed through in that promise. He sought peace before he went to war.

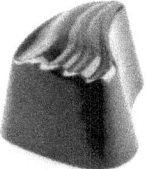

The Lord's Patience – Again

¹ Again the Israelites did evil in the Lord's sight, so the Lord handed them over to the Philistines, who oppressed them for forty years.

Judges 13:1

Samson is another warrior judge whom God has called to deliver his people. As this chapter opens, we hear a familiar note, a familiar tone. The Lord is going to *again* send deliverance. The Lord is going to *again* show patience. The Lord is going to *again* come to the rescue of his people because they have *again* sinned. They have *again* done evil in the sight of the Lord. And I want to spend some time on that word *again* right now because I want me and you to realize that in our lives the Lord *again* has rescued us. The Lord *again* has saved us from ourselves and our own silliness. The Lord *again* has established our going. The Lord *again* has moved us from situations in our lives that were troubling, that were even dangerous. *Again* shows his love. *Again* shows the character of God. Like the nation of God's people, we ourselves have moved away from the call of God many times and because of his long-suffering, *again* he comes to see about us.

Now, this particular judge of Israel has a unique beginning. An angelic visitor comes to see his mom and tells her, Even though you are a barren woman (she had not had a child up unto this point), you're going to be blessed with a child that's special. He's going to be special in his strength, special in his calling, and special in his ability to deliver the nation from the Philistines. This was a unique call in that he was called before he was born

to serve the Lord in this very special and supernatural way. What can we glean from that? God calls us, every one of us. You're called to a certain station in life. If you're a believer this morning, this afternoon, this evening, whenever you're reading this, God has called you. You were called before the foundations of the world were created by Almighty God. So, we have that in common with Samson.

Now the father didn't quite believe what his wife was telling him. Maybe she'd been out in the sun too long, he thought, maybe it was just that time of age for her and she wasn't thinking too clearly. He didn't know what was going on, but he did say, Next time the man from heaven comes, come get me, show me. Some of us don't believe until we see, but the Bible's very clear: blessed and happy, filled with ecstatic joy are those who believe without having necessarily to see with their eyes; those who launch out on faith. Well, the visitor came back and she got her husband and the angel gave her the same instruction, gave her a plan for prenatal care, not to drink strong drink, not to drink wine or even grape juice, or deal in anything that was going to hinder this fetus, this child, this young man. That prenatal care is still good today for expectant moms. There are certain things that you don't need to eat, don't need to drink, don't need to do. Prenatal care is important, both then and now.

God calls us, every one of us.

This was a going to be a child with a special destiny in life. Now, he was born and as he developed, as he became older, it was noted that he was different from other young men. He had power and that power of physical strength became known among the people that surrounded him. He was rambunctious, he was rebellious, if he was told to do one thing, he would do something totally different. Yet the Lord used him. Let's look at me and you for an example. We have agreed that we have a

calling on our lives. We also need to agree that there have been times when we have been rebellious, rambunctious, stubborn, arrogant, disobedient, but God came to our rescue *again*.

Think about this supernatural birth. My mother used to tell me that all births are a miracle of God, so that's something else you have in common with Samson. You are, and I am, a miracle of birth. Can't explain it any other way, you have a miracle in your beginning. The circumstance of your birth doesn't matter — it is yet a miracle because you're still here. You and I have *again*, at times, moved away from the doctrines and teaching of the Lord and, *again*, he has come to our rescue. Something else we have in common with Samson. We have walked the path contrary to the will of God, just like the nation of Israel was so many times, fickle. How has the Lord re-entered your life and *again* established your life? Wherever you are right now, you are there for the Lord to do something to you *again*, that's going to lift you up and deliver you.

Sweet Samples from Scripture

Pastor Walter Henry Cross

Responding to God's Call

Sweet Samples from Scripture

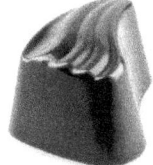

Pastor Walter Henry Cross

Are You Standing on Holy Turf?

¹ One day Moses was tending the flock of his father-in-law, Jethro, the priest of Midian. He led the flock far into the wilderness and came to Sinai, the mountain of God. ² There the angel of the Lord appeared to him in a blazing fire from the middle of a bush. Moses stared in amazement. Though the bush was engulfed in flames, it didn't burn up. ³ "This is amazing," Moses said to himself. "Why isn't that bush burning up? I must go see it." ⁴ When the Lord saw Moses coming to take a closer look, God called to him from the middle of the bush, "Moses! Moses!" "Here I am!" Moses replied. ⁵ "Do not come any closer," the Lord warned. "Take off your sandals, for you are standing on holy ground.

Exodus 3:1-5

Moses and the burning bush, that was a phenomenon that happened in the Old Testament, and our scripture of consideration today is in Exodus. Exodus means "the way out." Now the phenomenon was that there was a bush that was burning but didn't burn up. But before we talk about Moses standing in front of that bush, we need to go back and see how he got there. Moses, like the other judges we've been studying and some of the prophets that we will and have studied, had a miraculous beginning. Remember that we have said that me and you had a miraculous beginning, and that the Lord does wonders all the time. Moses was born in a time when it was dangerous for boys of his race, of his nationality, to be born because they would become, at least in the mind of those who were in charge, a threat to their very existence. So, Hebrew

baby boys were sought after to be murdered by the kings who were in charge, the Pharaohs, which was a title, not a name.

Now, Moses' mother was very wise. Our mothers have helped us to survive through all types of manner of danger. She was a wise woman; she had the wisdom of God. She looked at her son and said, You have that mark of destiny upon you, God's favor on your life. The Bible says that he was just a fine young man. His mother could tell his potential from infancy. So, she decided that she needed to hide him. Well, after about three months it became difficult to hide a baby, so she prepared a little boat, a basket, maybe even woven by her own hands. When she finished the basket, she put something that made it waterproof on the inside so it would float. Then she put something in there that would make it comfortable and give it some stability. Then she kissed her little baby goodbye and said, Lord he's in your hands. Down the river she sent him. Possibly she knew that the women of Egyptian royalty would find him in the river during their bathing time and take care of him. That may have been her hope, that may have been the way the Lord revealed it to her. But again, I go back to saying she was a wise woman.

Well, as God would have it, the Egyptian women found him and took him to their mistress. She said, I just can't stand for this baby to cry. She had compassion, she had mercy, and she took him to the palace to raise as her own. God worked this thing. We need to stop here long enough to say amen to God. Hasn't he worked some stuff in your life? I know he has in mine. He worked this thing, and when they sent for a nursing mother, it turned out that the mother of Moses was the one that was dispatched to the palace to take care of her own son. Only God, the God that we serve, can fix it like that. So, Moses was educated, he was prepared, he was royally treated, and he grew up in the palace.

Now, that Hebrew blood was still in Moses. That innate passion that God had put in him was still there and as he walked around the palace grounds, he had sympathy for the

people of God that were being mistreated. One day he saw a mean Egyptian, a foreman, like a field foreman, who was being brutal to some of Moses' own kinsmen. That family passion rose up in Moses and he killed the Egyptian foreman, or boss, then hid him in the sand and went about his business. Did God honor that? Did God tell him to do that? I don't think so. We've got rules and the same God that eventually gave the Ten Commandments was the same God that was with Moses at that time and did not authorize him to take matters into his own hands. Did Moses have to deal with the consequences? I think so. As we'll see, he ended up having to go to the backside of the desert for 40 years where God continued to deal with his anger management.

We need to stop here long enough to say amen to God. Hasn't he worked some stuff in your life?

Well the next day, as the story goes on, Moses was outside again, trying to create some type of rapport with his kinsmen because they were fussing and fighting. He interceded and said, Brother, you're wrong, don't hit your kinsman. And the brother turned to him saying, What are you going to do about it? Are you going to kill me like you killed that Egyptian yesterday? Moses said, Uh-oh, I've got to get out of here.

Now, why did Moses have to leave? He knew something was going to happen, he knew the word was going to get back to the Pharaoh because the Bible says that the Pharaoh found out and got mad and sought to kill Moses. Maybe Moses revealed his nationality because of his passion for justice. Maybe the princess, his stepmother, told the Pharaoh that he had little Hebrew blankets on him. Maybe the Pharaoh knew all the time, maybe he knew by the hue of Moses' skin and just ignored the fact that he looked like he was Hebrew. I don't know, but I know this: he sought to kill Moses and Moses had to leave.

That brings us to where today's story starts. Moses is out being a rancher. While he's tending his sheep one day, he has an opportunity to help some young women, some daughters of another rancher. One of the daughters that he helped told her daddy that this man had been very kind to them out in the field. And the father said, Bring him here, we're going to give him fellowship. In due process of time, this priest of Midian gave him one of his daughters to wed. So, Moses was doing all right, he was a family man, he was a rancher.

Our prayers, our tears, are not going unheard by the God of heaven that we serve.

One day when he was walking, he didn't see a flash of lightning and he didn't hear an explosion, but something grabbed his attention. That something was that there was a bush a-burning. Now this is a desert-like area and it wasn't unusual to see spontaneous combustion. But this fire did not consume the bush. Wouldn't that grab your attention? If you set a piece of newspaper on fire, pretty soon you just have some white ashes, some white powder because the fire is consuming, and it will continue to burn as long as there's fuel. Well, the bush was fuel and the fire was raging but not a leaf fell off, nothing turned brown, nothing turned black. Probably there was no smoke because there was nothing being consumed. This got the attention of Moses and the Lord spoke through the bush and told him, You are my deliverer. I know you have a passion for your brothers and sisters. I know your heart aches for the pain that they're going through. I have heard your prayer, I have heard the cry of my people. Now, it's very important for us to know that God hears us when we pray, and that God understands the pain that me and you are dealing with at this very moment. Our prayers, our tears, are not going unheard by the God of heaven that we serve. We need to know that.

Well, you know rest the story about Moses becoming the great deliverer and how God used the plagues to get them out of Egypt. Some of us are still stuck in Egypt. Some of us still think it's better off in slavery than it is being free and independent and living for God. I don't know where we get that from, but some of us act like we're more at home in slavery, more at home in sin, than we are living for the Lord. So Moses became the great deliverer. He put up a whole lot of excuses at first and said he couldn't talk. So God gave him Aaron to talk, but we never see where Aaron went to talk to the Pharaoh. As long as Moses was around, Moses did all the talking. Moses offered one excuse after another, but God called him, and he went. Now, let's go back to the bush. That's where we are going to stop. What does God have to do this morning to get your attention? Is he going to have to set somebody on fire in your life? Some preacher, some psalmist, some usher, some deacon, some Sunday school teacher? Watch them burn as God speaks through them. The fire of the Lord won't consume them, but you need to stand still and know, as Moses was instructed, that this is holy ground. When you see God set somebody on fire, you have been invited into a sacred space and the Lord is speaking to you through that event. What does God have to do to get your attention? What does he have to set on fire in your life and in my life? When you see God burning somewhere, listen — you are on holy turf.

Sweet Samples from Scripture

Pastor Walter Henry Cross

Are You Willing to Go?

⁵ Then I said, "It's all over! I am doomed, for I am a sinful man. I have filthy lips, and I live among a people with filthy lips. Yet I have seen the King, the Lord of Heaven's Armies." ⁶ Then one of the seraphim flew to me with a burning coal he had taken from the altar with a pair of tongs. ⁷ He touched my lips with it and said, "See, this coal has touched your lips. Now your guilt is removed, and your sins are forgiven." ⁸ Then I heard the Lord asking, "Whom should I send as a messenger to this people? Who will go for us?" I said, "Here I am. Send me."

Isaiah 6:5-8

Today, let's read about Isaiah. Isaiah was a prophet who was called by God to deliver a message to God's people. We define a prophet as one who speaks forth the truth. That's his assignment. That's his or her calling. There can be male or female prophets speaking forth the truth. The utterance of God is given to him or her by God. Now, during the time of Isaiah's prophecy, he had served through four kings, some good, some not so good. The nation was divided; God's people were divided between the northern kingdom and the southern kingdom. They were not doing well; idolatry and immorality were sweeping the land. The people had divided into a southern camp and a northern camp. Ten tribes to the north and two to the south.

Almighty God had given them their final warning. The northern group of the people of God did not heed, they did not pay

attention to what God was saying. We know that even God has a time limit, so then they were dispersed according to the prophecy. As God had pre-warned them, they were taken away into captivity and never again would be a symbol as a nation. Prophetically, when Jesus comes back, there will be an opportunity for some of those in the northern tribes to again have fellowship with Almighty God. Isaiah's focus was the southern kingdom, where Jerusalem is. Judea, or the house of Judah, which was made up of two tribes, were not much better than the northern group. They were involved in idolatry; anything that looked good, smelled good, tasted good, they ran after it. Their neighbors would have a certain type of worship and they desired it. A certain fashion, a certain fad, a certain type of anything and we will just run after it. See, there's not a lot of difference between the people of God then and the people of God now. We are subject to stray from the precepts and teachers of the Lord to anything that comes by.

Isaiah is known as the prince of the prophets and the reason he is called that is because he was so accurate. He gives such a splendid and clear picture of the birth of Jesus Christ, of the death and suffering of Jesus Christ, and the return of Jesus Christ. He is very clear in his prophetic utterance. As Isaiah 6 opens, Isaiah's in the temple, and he's tired. He's tired of all the sin and he's tired of all the confusion. He's tired of all the backbiting and back and forth and he's humbled in the presence of the Lord, praying for his nation. That's something that we could be doing, right? Praying for our nation? Isaiah was humbled by the circumstances that have brought the late nation so low and so far away from God Jehovah. Then suddenly an angelic being, or celestial being would be a better term, showed up and this being allowed Isaiah to know that he was in the presence of Almighty God. Isaiah looked up and saw the throne room of heaven and that affected him, being in that area of glory and sacredness changed him. Suddenly, the angel took a coal off the coal pile in heaven, the same way it's designed in the temple, and flew across the room and touched

Isaiah's lips. At that point he became aware that God was using him.

Now, the contrast here is that when he saw the holiness of God, when he saw the righteousness of God, when he saw the glory of God, he looked at himself and the people of God and he saw non-compliance, he saw sin, he saw darkness, he saw the power of Satan pushing them ever away from the presence of God, and he didn't like it. He said, Woe is me. He said, Look how bad I am. We need to look at how bad we are. Until we see where we are, we're not going to get any better. Until we recognize that we are dependent on sin and the substance of sin, until we recognize we could be better than we are, until we recognize we have walked away from the power of God and been taken over by the power of sin, until we recognize where we are, we cannot do any better. We certainly cannot be in full fellowship with the Lord.

Well, Isaiah recognized that. The touching of the lips with the coal from heaven symbolizes cleansing, sanctification, being set aside for the use of God. It symbolizes ordination, approval from heaven that your sins are now forgiven. Forgiveness is available. If you're reading this, forgiveness is available. If you say yes right now, the Lord, with sin-cleansing power through the blood of Jesus Christ will turn you around. Well, the next thing that happened was that the Lord said, I need somebody. I need someone to warn, to encourage, to bring hope, to talk about the results of sin, to talk about the future and the present. I need a spokesperson.

Now, we've read about Moses and we've read about some of the other judges that were leaders and were reluctant. We know that we ourselves are reluctant to heed the call of God. We understand that. Did Isaiah pull back? Did he say, Lord find somebody else? No! Isaiah gave that famous, thunderous reply, Lord, here am I, send me! And the Lord did. The Lord sent him as a voice of warning, woe to you; a voice of encouragement, the Messiah's coming; a voice of hope, it won't always be like this.

All of the people of God would not be destroyed. But those of you who have decided to go your own way and gone so far from the fire that you've grown cold, may the Lord have mercy on your souls.

Think about the call of Isaiah. Are you willing to let the Lord purge you of sin? I'm not talking about going through a ceremony. I'm talking about allowing the forgiving power of God to renew you, to restore you, to energize you, to cleanse you, to make you worthy. Remember where Isaiah was. He was in a worshipping mode. Even though his heart was sorrowful for the people and conditions of the land, he was in the place of worship. Get in that place of worship this morning. Let yourself be touched by the fire of Almighty God. Let your hand be raised and say, Lord here am I. Send me. I'll go. How many are willing to go? How many are willing to accept that challenge? I don't know where the Lord is going to send you. I don't know where he's going to tell you to go or what he's going to tell you to do. That's not the point. The point is, are you willing to serve God in such a way that you will give Him glory and honor?

Pastor Walter Henry Cross

God Will Provide

¹³ Then Abraham looked up and saw a ram caught by its horns in a thicket. So he took the ram and sacrificed it as a burnt offering in place of his son. ¹⁴ Abraham named the place Yahweh-Yireh (which means "the Lord will provide"). To this day, people still use that name as a proverb: "On the mountain of the Lord it will be provided."

Genesis 22:13-14

Let's talk about Isaac and his father, Abraham. Now you know this story pretty well, how Abram was given a promise by God and God gave him the faith to trust in him. So Abram became Abraham and he began his journey of becoming the father of a mighty nation. The word *testing* is part of this story. God does not, according to James 1:13 attempt to coerce us to do evil for any reason. That's not the nature of God. But the idea of testing is part of the nature of God. Testing makes us strong. It helps us to develop, it helps us to learn and to retain. So, I'm going to press that idea just a moment, this testing idea.

The first test we see in our story was the call to leave home. Abram had a call from God to go into a place that he did not know. That's a test and God gave him imputed righteousness in the faith to follow that test. So Abram has gone to another area and God comes back again for another examination. The first examination was the entrance exam. The second examination was the midterm. God says, I'm going to give you

a son. Abraham and his wife said, No, we're too old for that kind of carrying on, Lord, I don't know how you're going to do this. And the Lord said, Just be patient it's going to be done. Believe me, Sunday school scholars, whatever the Lord said he's going to do, it will be done. We have to have the faith to trust him because the Lord God that we serve is a provider.

Well, they got impatient, Abraham his wife, Sarah. They got impatient and decide that they would go another route to achieve what God had already promised them. Abraham failed the midterm exam. He didn't do well. And after a lot of confusion and suffering and doing things out of the will of God, a child came into life that was not the promised son. This happened because of disobedience and impatient and trying to help God out. How many of us know today that God doesn't need us to help him out?

So now we come to the graduation or the final exam. After all that trouble of having a son the wrong way, they have Isaac. Beautiful little Isaac. Isaac begins to grow up in the admonition and the love of family and God. He's being taught all these wonderful things. He's seeing his father and his mother worship God. And at some point in time, probably as a tweener, somewhere between nine and thirteen, Isaac's father says to him, Let's go and make a sacrifice. The Lord has told me I need to do this. So, they pack up their animal and get provisions for the sacrifice, the wood, the knife, and the fire. They bring two assistants along with them and they go on a three-day journey to an area known as Moriah which is in a region of mountains close to Jerusalem. And they begin the journey up Mount Moriah.

Isaac is very bright, he's very aware and he asks his dad, You have fire, I have the wood, you've got the knife, but where is the lamb? Now we learn something from this exchange. We can tell the heart of Abraham is sorrowful but his will is to please God. He goes right on indicating to his son that God will provide. Well, they get up on the mountaintop and he ties his son up.

Now at this point, since Abraham is a man of age, I think it would have been possible that Isaac, who had toted that wood up the mountain, probably could have subdued his father. But out of obedience he submits to the will of his father. They build up a little altar, they scatter the wood, and he ties up his son. Abraham pulls the knife back to slit Isaac's throat and prepare for the sacrifice. And at that moment, you know God's never late, at that moment there's a rustling in the bushes and there's a ram. An angel tells Abraham, Don't harm your child; God has provided a ram. Abraham takes the ram and prepares it for the sacrifice. He passes his final exam.

When you don't know what you're going to do next, trust God.

We need to understand that God is a provider. At times, it may seem like the time sequence for our comfort is all out of whack. When you don't know what you're going to do next, trust God. When you're facing your Mount Moriah of opportunity, trust God. When it comes time for you to do something that you are not real sure about, at that point trust God. Listen for his voice because God is a provider. Now let's look at some interesting similarities. Mount Moriah was in one of the mountain ranges that surrounds Jerusalem and it was probably the range that included Mount Calvary. Isaac, the son, carried the wood up the mountain. Jesus, the Son, carried the cross up the mountain. Isaac was bound and laid on the wood. Jesus was spiked and riveted and laid on the wood. But here's a little nugget of difference. God did not spare his only Son. God spared the life of Abraham's only son. God went the extra mile of the way to provide salvation for us.

At that very moment when it looks like all hope is lost in our lives, there may be a rustling in the bushes. Think about those times in your life when it looked like there was no hope and

then there was a rustling in the bushes, a sound of victory, a sound and a sign of provision. It was a time when it was the due date for something in life and God provided. It was time to pay those college tuition fees, and God provided. It was time to go to the cupboard one more time even though you knew there was not another can in there, but somehow God provided. Celebrate that today. Celebrate how God keeps on providing for us. God will, God has, and he will again, bless us beyond our wildest imagination if we will only trust him.

Not Ability, But Availability

⁶ "O Sovereign Lord," I said, "I can't speak for you! I'm too young!"

⁷ The Lord replied, "Don't say, 'I'm too young,' for you must go wherever I send you and say whatever I tell you. ⁸ And don't be afraid of the people, for I will be with you and will protect you. I, the Lord, have spoken!" ⁹ Then the Lord reached out and touched my mouth and said, "Look, I have put my words in your mouth! ¹⁰ Today I appoint you to stand up against nations and kingdoms. Some you must uproot and tear down, destroy and overthrow. Others you must build up and plant."

Jeremiah 1:6-10

Let's talk about the call of the prophet Jeremiah. We've had some fascinating call stories lately and you might wonder why we're continuing to talk about this. Well, God may be talking to you, he may be talking to me, he may be talking to us because I want to assure you that everyone who reads this has a call on their life, every single one. We get confused because sometimes we like to think of a call as being in the pulpit and wearing the liturgical robes and the stoles around the neck, or going to a foreign country to do something that's kingdom-building. But from where you are sitting right now to where you are going to be in the next twenty minutes or the next two hours represents an opportunity for you to be a minister of light in the kingdom of God here on earth. So, this call story is for you.

In the first verse of Jeremiah it says *the words of Jeremiah.* Later on it says *the words of the Lord came to Jeremiah.* That's

what we're used to hearing, the words of the Lord coming to a certain prophet or speaker. It makes you wonder what the difference is between the words of Jeremiah and the words of the Lord that the Lord would have Jeremiah to say. Here is what the difference is. The words of Jeremiah encase, or encapsulate, the words of the Lord, plus Jeremiah's observation of the times. Christian leaders must be observant of the present time and the present culture. In order to speak truth to the culture, we need to be aware of it. Now we don't necessarily have to be participants in the evil of the world, but we need to be consciously aware of what's going on in the world around us in order to minister to it.

Jeremiah was that type of prophet and the words of Jeremiah talk about how he observed what was going on in the culture, how the northern tribe had turned their back on God and had gone after other nations and other gods. During his narrative he often used the illustration of immorality and idolatrous together because it is an immoral thing to follow other gods. Let me tell you this. When you lose contact with God, one of the first items on Satan's menu is immorality. When God is not your God, and something or someone else occupies that space, the first temptation is immorality. Bear that in mind.

Jeremiah came from a priestly household. He knew the ways of the Lord from a small child. As he receives his call, we realize that he was a young man because he says, How can I speak these words as truth? They're not going to hear me, they're not going to pay me any attention, I'm too young, I don't have enough voice. He was not necessarily talking about volume but about experience and how he looked in the eyes of others. That's also a hindrance to us being all that we can be for the Lord, because we are concerned, worried about, or have a sense of anxiety about how other people view us. They won't hear me; I don't have any letters behind my name or in front. They won't hear me; I come from across the tracks. They won't hear me; I don't look the part. But God told Jeremiah, Don't worry about

any of that, don't be afraid of their faces, don't be intimidated, don't be beat down. You have a difficult message to share; a message of warning and impending danger and destruction, but you also have a message of hope. To give both of these messages out, I'm going to be with you. I will speak for you.

What God is looking for from us is not a whole lot of what we would characterize as ability, he's looking for availability. Then he will give the giftedness. He will give you the words to say and how to say them. He'll give you that dynamic spirit-led timing. God will even tell you when not to talk when you are dependent upon him. Again, we see this illustration; God says it again so we can really hear it this time in case we missed it before. Remember how Isaiah's lips were purified from off the altar with the hot coal? Now God himself touches the lips of Jeremiah. Again, this is a signal, this is a sign of approval, this is a sign of ordination, this is a sign of God sanctifying this individual to be used in kingdom-building.

If you would and if I would make ourselves available to Almighty God, he will touch us again and again and give us that power of the Holy Spirit to accomplish whatever he wants us to do, whatever he's calling us to. I want you to think about how God has set you aside to do his work. I want you to discover if God has called you and you might have said, Say what? Think about how you can be more available to the Lord, telling him, I'm available to you. We need to live that out.

We need to hear the cry of Jeremiah. Here's another thought. Oftentimes we've heard that Jeremiah was the weeping prophet, that his eyes were full of tears. I want to add a little bit to that. The scripture does bear out the fact that he did shed many tears. He was passionate, he was a passionate prophet. And if we're not brought to tears by the sin and the degradation of this world, we do not have the passion that we need to spread the word of God. We ought to care. We ought to care sufficiently enough that we are driven to our knees, that we cry. But here's the key: then we've got to get up and do something about

it. Crying's not effective if you're not going to be moved with passionate love enough to do something about poverty, hunger, injustice. If we're not going to do something about it, crying won't help. Jeremiah cried but as the song says, he cried his last tear. Then he got up and told the truth about God. Are you challenged? Are you ready? Let's go.

Pastor Walter Henry Cross

Eat the Whole Roll

¹ The voice said to me, "Son of man, eat what I am giving you—eat this scroll! Then go and give its message to the people of Israel." ² So I opened my mouth, and he fed me the scroll. ³ "Fill your stomach with this," he said. And when I ate it, it tasted as sweet as honey in my mouth.

⁴ Then he said, "Son of man, go to the people of Israel and give them my messages. ⁵ I am not sending you to a foreign people whose language you cannot understand. ⁶ No, I am not sending you to people with strange and difficult speech. If I did, they would listen! ⁷ But the people of Israel won't listen to you any more than they listen to me! For the whole lot of them are hard-hearted and stubborn. ⁸ But look, I have made you as obstinate and hard-hearted as they are. ⁹ I have made your forehead as hard as the hardest rock! So don't be afraid of them or fear their angry looks, even though they are rebels."

Ezekiel 3:1-9

Ezekiel was another prophet of the Lord, one who speaks forth the truth to God's people and also warns all people about the power of God, the punishment of God, the provision of God, the protection of God, and just who God is if they are willing to listen. We're going to focus briefly on part of chapter three of the book of Ezekiel. As the picture opens, Ezekiel is having a vision. He's been called from a priestly household to go and tell the people of God what God has said. There had been an attack in the southern kingdom and part of the people have been taken away into

slavery. During this particular vision, Ezekiel is flown away by the power and the glory of God to minister to the people who are already in exile.

Now this picture is awesome; he's under a tree, he's upset because the people of God have been so disobedient, and the punishment of God was now coming upon them. Then he sees something. It looks like a storm but when it gets closer, he recognizes that it is the glory of God, the awesomeness of God. He does the best he can with human eyes and human words to describe it. We understand that he sees a roll, a scroll, a piece of paper that's rolled up with words written on the front side and on the back side. A voice comes and Ezekiel acknowledges that it is the voice of God. Ezekiel is full of reverence at the voice of God and he bows down and prostrates himself in front of this glorious appearance. The Lord says, Get up, take this scroll, this roll, this document with words written on it, words of lamentations, words of sadness, words of sorrow because the people have been so corrupt and disobedient. Now, I want you to take the word of the Lord and ingest them into your body. Yes, I want you to eat them. And Ezekiel, probably like we would do, says, Say what? Yes, I want you to eat them.

So we usually don't eat paper and print as a habit. But look at Ezekiel. The Lord tells him to do something that's extraordinary, that's out of the realm of the ordinary, and he does it. And he says, the words on this paper, on this scroll, that I am ingesting are sweet to me. He uses the phrase honey. That's significant because honey was valuable and rare. Maybe they didn't have as many flowers as we have but whatever the reason, honey was reserved for the royalty. Different type of sweeteners that we have today, like cane sugar and guava, were not as prominent in that area so honey was valuable and was reserved for people who could afford it. One place in the Bible talks about honey being like gold. So, it tastes like honey, it was sweet. What was sweet about it? We know that it had words of lamentation and sorrow on it, so what was sweet about eating the word of God?

The sweetness was Ezekiel's obedience, his faithfulness, his ability to adhere to what God was saying. God said eat it and he chomped down on it.

The symbolism behind ingesting the Word of God is very strong. Pay attention to that. Ezekiel is a very, very symbolic book, a book that's filled with imagery and you can get fascinated by trying to figure out and decipher the code, as if you were looking at a movie or a video game. Don't get so involved in the imagery that you forget the message or you miss the message. The message is, if God said it, be faithful and obedient. Ezekiel ate the roll. Now this became food in his stomach and in the innermost part of his being. The word for stomach, for the intestinal system in the Old Testament, also referred to the heart. In our language it would refer to our mind, to the innermost being of our consciousness, our conscience, our awareness. In other words, we need to get the word on the inside. You cannot tell anybody about what you don't know. You cannot share light that you don't already have. We need to get the word on the inside. We need to believe that the Bible is right. We need to know what the Bible stands for, what it says. We need to be able to explain it as if we have a reason for hope within us that the Bible says is the very Word of God. We need to get it on the inside.

Now, during this vision, Ezekiel is lifted up and taken away, and he's put down in the middle of captivity. God was showing him that he would be taken away by soldiers and would serve in a foreign place, the palace in Babylon, and that God would want him to talk to his people there in captivity with him, and tell them about the dangers of disobedience, telling them what God told him to say. God shared some other things with him and one of the things that God said was, They're not going to hear you but I want you to talk to your people, the people that speak the same language. If I sent you to a foreign country to speak to the leaders and the people of that country, you would have a language barrier, but you would still be more successful dealing

with the people with the language barrier than you will be with your own kinsmen.

How is that true in our lives? Some of the hardest people to evangelize, to disciple, to speak words of truth and deliverance to, to talk common sense to, are some of our own relatives. Some of the people in our own house just won't hear us. That's what the Lord is telling Ezekiel. So why, you may ask, why would the Lord send him? Why would the Lord go through all this trouble? Because the Lord is loving, and He is just. No one is going to their own condemnation without a just God providing them a way out, providing them a sign and the hope of truth.

The book of Ezekiel is the one that talks about the wheel in the middle of the wheel and the dry bones in the valley; a lot of preaching comes out of Ezekiel. But, like I said, don't get the imagery mixed up with the essence of the message. Eat the word, the whole word, don't cherry-pick it. Don't go around telling people you're a New Testament Christian; you're a Bible Christian. Don't tell people that you just believe in the formal part of the Bible; you're a Bible Christian. What did the word say? Eat the whole roll. We need to live by the whole Bible. Jesus was very clear. He didn't do away with any of the Bible. He brought it together in beautiful harmony into himself. Consume the word, consume righteousness, and then go and tell the people of God the truth about God.

Think about some of the hard things that the Lord has asked you to do that turned out okay. Something real difficult, something that didn't make sense to you in the beginning, but after you paid attention and you were obedient to it, it worked out well, it turned out to be a blessing. Let me challenge you: if you're faced with a decision right now and it's difficult, if you understand that the Lord is leading you into an area that's strange to you, do it. If God said it, it'll be verified in his word. Do it and then one day you'll stand, maybe in Sunday school, maybe in church, maybe in your own household, and testify to the goodness of the Lord.

Pastor Walter Henry Cross

There Is Hope

¹⁴ But Amos replied, "I'm not a professional prophet, and I was never trained to be one. I'm just a shepherd, and I take care of sycamore-fig trees. ¹⁵ But the Lord called me away from my flock and told me, 'Go and prophesy to my people in Israel.'

Amos 7:14-15

Most of us are familiar with Amos and Andy. We're going to talk about an Amos without the Andy. Amos is a biblical character who was a prophet. He is referred to as a minor prophet, not because his message was less important than any of the other prophets, but because the book that was attributed to him was shorter. As we go into Amos, we want to focus on chapter seven, but prior to getting there, this writer wrote about gloom and doom, he wrote about pending destruction, he wrote about being scattered, famine, fire, he wrote about war, he wrote about defeat, he wrote about death, blood, and gore — such violence. Makes you wonder, what was the Lord's purpose in all of this? Well, as we have studied the other prophets, we have found out that the Lord is patient, merciful, and kind. Now, how does that equate with the Book of Amos? Amos, again, is demonstrating how the Lord God was patient with his people, the people of the northern kingdom and the southern kingdom. But, finally, the Lord had enough. Repeatedly in the Book of Amos, and you'll hear this three and four times, I have warned you, I have punished you, I have encouraged you, I have spoken the truth

to you in love. But you have disobeyed and gone after foreign gods, you have committed atrocities even in the temple of the holy God.

Now, students, scholars, whoever you are, God has a time limit set for me and you. He will not always tolerate our evil and our idolatry. You may say God's a loving God. Well, a loving God disciplines. And God is the only God and he disciplines. You discipline your children because you love them. Now, God has told the northern kingdom, if you keep living the way you are, destruction is going to be at hand. So, we see it's truth time. It's time for their laundry ticket to get punched. It's time for the Lord to do what he said he was going to do. As parents, as grandparents, as leaders, don't keep saying the same thing with no action. If you say it, if you promise it, do it. That means that you are effective in parenting and leadership.

You may say God's a loving God. Well, a loving God disciplines.

Look at this in your life and in my life. We have promised the Lord so much. We have repented. We have said, Lord, if you save me, I'll serve you. But so many times all of us, and that includes me, and whoever is reading this, we have gotten up from our beds of affliction, from our crises, from our tragedies, from our confusion and, after the Lord has blessed us, we have gone home and sat on our seat of do nothing and said, Lord, catch me if you can. Don't turn away. Somebody may think I'm talking about them, but I'm not. I'm talking about all of us who have been like the northern kingdom and have gone away from God. We need an Amos in our lives who will cry aloud and tell the truth. The Lord is coming. But even at this point, if you repent sincerely, the Lord will relent that punishment against you.

Now, who is Amos? Amos, by his own admission, his own resume, says, I am a herdsman and a picker of fruit. He did not come across as being a person of any particular pedigree in terms of his schooling, his background, or his heritage. He was a noble farmer and herdsman and he would cultivate fruit trees, but God called him and used him mightily. We talked about this before; God does not have a pecking order. He may and can call me and you. Now in my case, he called me, and I'm sure that was amusing to some people, and it liked to scare me to death. But God can use anybody who's willing and available. So, from following herds and picking fruit, Amos was assigned to go to the northern kingdom and blow the trumpet of warning. He was to tell the people, this time the Lord is going to do what he told you he was going to do all the time. He's going to scatter you, going to divide you, you're going to be defeated. The difference is that you're not coming back home this time. It's over. Now for the little southern kingdom, God's going to give you another chance. You're going to be punished, it's going to be severe, it's going to be harsh, but there will be a remnant. Up to the mathematical point of 90% are going to be annihilated, but God will take the 10% and return them to the land. And they are there today.

What can we gather from Amos? He was criticized. The royalty of the north said, go home, you agitator. Here's something Amos used to do. He used to go to the curb market. He used to watch the merchants at the flea market. They would put their thumb on the scale and Amos would tell on them. He would tell them, you are fleecing the people, you are taking their hard-earned money, you are taking people into slavery. And then Amos would tell the story of God's righteousness and God's patience and God's judgment.

We see all of this in the power of Almighty God in our lives. God is doing what is right, what is just and what is necessary for his name to be holy. What has God done in your life? Have you received an Amos warning in your life? Did you heed

what were the consequences? Or are you at the brink now of annihilation because you're stubborn, obstinate, you're mean-spirited, you've got that don't-care attitude? Amos said, The Lord's got your number. But there is hope. If you say yes to the Lord, the end of the book of Amos says that the war fields are going to be turned into a garden of plenty. God will restore the land that the locust has destroyed. God will restore your life if you want to leave sin and walk in the marvelous light. Amos says to me and to you, God is waiting on you.

Pastor Walter Henry Cross

Meeting the Needs

¹ But as the believers rapidly multiplied, there were rumblings of discontent. The Greek-speaking believers complained about the Hebrew-speaking believers, saying that their widows were being discriminated against in the daily distribution of food. ² So the Twelve called a meeting of all the believers. They said, "We apostles should spend our time teaching the word of God, not running a food program. ³ And so, brothers, select seven men who are well respected and are full of the Spirit and wisdom. We will give them this responsibility. ⁴ Then we apostles can spend our time in prayer and teaching the word."

Acts 6:1-4

Let's talk again about God's call to us. Yes, the reason for these series of call stories and call situations is to let us know that God is still calling men and women, boys and girls into kingdom-action. As a minister of the gospel, I have surrendered my life to the call of the Lord, but you know what? The Lord is still calling me. He's still calling you. Different situations come up in life and it's not unusual for the Lord to call us to do something that may be different than we thought, or it may be deeper than we we've gone, or it may be out wider than we ever intended to go. But keep listening, keep on listening, God is yet calling.

Let's go to the book of Acts, the book that gives a historic account of the actions of the new church, the embryonic church, and of the apostles as they made their way through the beginning of a new era of the gospel. Let's take a look at chapter 6. Jesus has gone, he's now on the right hand of his Father. The

apostles had been given their marching orders at the mountain of Ascension and now they're going into all the world and all of Judea to tell about the goodness of Jesus Christ, the good news of Jesus Christ, the freedom of Jesus Christ which is the gospel. We see them as the scene opens today; they have been involved in this mission of ministry and freedom and going against the prevailing culture. They didn't set out to go against the culture, it's just that in telling the truth about Jesus, oftentimes you'll find yourself in opposition to the prevailing culture. Take care to speak the truth in love and keep on keepin' on. Don't stop, don't give in, don't give out, don't turn around, don't go back. Keep on moving toward the prize that the Father has given us through his Son Jesus Christ empowered by the person and the presence of the Holy Spirit.

> **They didn't set out to go against the culture, it's just that in telling the truth about Jesus, oftentimes you'll find yourself in opposition to the prevailing culture.**

The disciples, the apostles, they had been students, now they're special messengers, and they are preaching. They are telling the truth and there comes a situation. Something has cropped up amongst this vast metropolitan congregation. There were some individuals, some women of Grecian heritage that were not native to the area where the apostles were preaching. They believed sincerely — they weren't making stuff up — that when the communal society that was part of the embryonic Church distributed food on the curb market day, on the bread day, they believed that when they got in line, their part had been picked over and they were only getting what was left. That was their perception. Now we won't get into a theological or historical argument or debate over whether there really was a shortage toward them, a slight toward them, or if it was actually true that the

men and women who were distributing food were purposely ignoring the Grecian women. What we want to underline and outline and circle is that it is the way they felt. A perception to a person is reality when we're dealing with each other. When we're dealing with individuals and they present you with a perception, a personal perception, don't always debate it, because that is their reality. What we want to do is work to resolve the issue according to their reality.

Now, notice the wisdom of the apostles. It is not good for us to stop preaching, to just stop praying, to stop studying and preparing ourselves to do the work of the Lord, and to get so involved in settling this dispute that we cannot do ministry. Look among yourselves. That was empowering the people. That's a good idea, leaders, empowering the people. Look among yourselves. You all know each other, find someone that you think is fair, that you think is full of integrity, and, here's the key, that you think is full of the Holy Spirit. Now if you've got the Holy Spirit, you're going to have fairness and integrity, and you're going to be gifted with wisdom. Look among yourselves and see who are the individuals that you would want to have rule over this matter. That way we don't have to turn to the business of distributing food and away from distributing the Word of God.

Notice that they took the time to meet the needs of the people. You've heard this and I still believe it's true, it's very hard for a man or a woman, or a boy or a girl to hear the word of God if their stomach is growling louder than the preacher or the missionary or the teacher. We need to attend to the needs of the people. We are called to hear the needs of the people, not to debate whether their needs are authentic or not. And we need to respond. Sometimes information is what they really need. Sometimes referral is what they need. And sometimes we need to put action on our words and attend to their various needs. The disciples made a very wise choice, led by the Holy Spirit, and the establishment of the deacon ministry came about. That word, deacon, means servant.

We are called to serve each other in the church and out of the church. We are called to hear the cry of those who feel disenfranchised, those who feel that they have been slighted. Not to debate whether that's real or not but to roll up our sleeves, go where they are, and do something about it. Then we are free to preach, then we are free to speak, then the church becomes a type of place that people want to be because they know that we care. And people don't know that we care until we care. They don't know that we're willing to give of our heart until we give of our substance, the two go hand-in-hand. I don't care how religious you are, if you are stingy, that's ultra-frugal, that's more than thrifty, it has a connotation of selfishness; if you are a miser, that's not the Spirit of God. Be wise, look around you, hear what the people say. Attempt, led by the Holy Spirit, to meet that need. Then you're free to teach and preach the gospel.

Think about the call that came upon the Apostles. It fell upon their ear that there was a need in the community. Think about the way they went about to solve it. Look at the leadership principles, how they instructed the people to look among themselves, how they utilized the wisdom of the people, how they dealt with cultural differences between the Grecian women and others, and how they brought the family of the church, the family of God, together and led that problem toward a positive resolution. What can we do, what can you do, what can I do to bring about resolution in a situation so that we are free to teach the Word of God?

Pastor Walter Henry Cross

Be a Living Epistle

³⁴ The eunuch asked Philip, "Tell me, was the prophet talking about himself or someone else?" ³⁵ So beginning with this same Scripture, Philip told him the Good News about Jesus. ³⁶ As they rode along, they came to some water, and the eunuch said, "Look! There's some water! Why can't I be baptized?" ³⁸ He ordered the carriage to stop, and they went down into the water, and Philip baptized him.

Acts 8:34-38

The church, the ecclesia, the called out ones, had some growing pains. This embryonic start of a new way of doing things in the religious community of the Jews and of embracing those who were outside of the Jewish nation and faith had some stumbles. Some problems are good to have. If you've got people standing around your sanctuary this morning, that's a good problem to have. Don't get too excited or in too much of a hurry to see what kind of building plan you're going to build. What kind of word are you going to build within these people who are already coming? Now, as Acts chapter 8 opens, we learn that believers had had more than one role. They also were ministers of the gospel. That brings me to this: you may be a deacon, which means servant, but you may also be called to do things in ministry other than serve. I don't think a good deacon is an individual who can only do the deacon ministry and forgets all other ministries. I don't think a pastor or a preacher can only do the preaching, and can't serve the people. We are called upon, in the church,

to do whatever the Lord wants us to do. We are called to meet the needs of the people.

The chapter opens up with the wave of persecution that came after Stephen's death. Stephen had been a tremendous gospel preacher of freedom in Jesus Christ. But the prevailing culture that consisted of the Roman Government and the elites of the Jewish community, those who were intimidated by the presence of this movement called The Way colluded to get rid of Stephen as they had already gotten rid of Jesus. They said, if we get rid of Stephen, these crowds will quit coming. But what happened as soon as they got rid of Stephen? Everything seemed to be going wrong for the church, but the crowds kept coming. The apostles stayed in Jerusalem. they refused to be intimidated and they kept on preaching. Philip was one of the original deacons and he was called to take on the mantle of preaching and doing many miraculous things. And the crowds kept coming.

Well, the Lord told Philip to go south. There's no indication that there was a discussion. Lord why, when, why me, why now? There's no indication that there was discussion. There was an assignment from the Lord and there was a sense of obedience from Philip. Leaders, scholars, when there's a word from the Lord, where is our obedience? He went south. Guided by the Lord through the Holy Spirit, Philip encountered a man sitting by the side of the road. He could tell by the design of the chariot that this was no ordinary man. He could look at his robe, his clothing, his entourage, and tell this was no ordinary man.

Everything seemed to be going wrong for the church, but the crowds kept coming.

This was a young man traveling up from North Africa and he was interested in the word of God. In fact, he had a copy of the word of God. He was in the right place at the right time, and he had the right information, but he was void of understanding.

There are people in our church today who are in the right place, they have the latest copy of the Word of God, they've got it on their phones, they've got it on their iPads, they've got all the information but they are void, empty of understanding.

This is where ministry comes into play. The Lord said, Run, get up in the chariot with him. Philip did that and asked the man, do you understand what you're reading? The man said no. I'm reading this ancient story of someone who was executed for preaching truth to God's people. Is Isaiah talking about himself or is he talking about another? Philip said, well, I'm glad you asked me. Then Philip told him the whole story about Jesus Christ. While they were riding along the roads, the man said, here is much water. Can I be baptized? He was baptized.

There are some interesting things in today's lesson. First of all, the word of God was prevalent in North Africa a long time before missionaries ever got there because this man knew about it. One thing that we know about this person is that he was a eunuch. That means that he was given a gift to be a person of loyalty. Now this gift was given to him either by God or by the hand of man, and it meant that he could work without an interruption of another focus on whatever his assignment was. This man was the treasurer of his nation. He was in a position of trust, so he had to be a person that was trustworthy. Somehow the Lord had reached him with the word of God, so he probably was bilingual. He probably dealt in investments for his Queen. He may have been a metropolitan, cosmopolitan person, but he was interested in the word. And the Lord gave him a sense of understanding through the ministry of Philip.

There are some people around you who may have a nice looking Bible, they may have commentaries and a library of information on their phone or their tablet, but they need you for understanding. They need your testimony, they need your exegesis of the word, they need your presence. How can you become a living epistle and care for others? How can you be

that person that they can ask the vital question to help them understand? From the cradle to the teenage years, they may ask, can you help me to understand? Are you ready to answer that question? Are you ready to give a reasonable answer for anyone who would ask you a question about the Gospel? Think of some innovative ways that you can come alive and make the word alive for others.

Has the Lord Changed Your Name?

13 "But Lord," exclaimed Ananias, "I've heard many people talk about the terrible things this man has done to the believers in Jerusalem! 14 And he is authorized by the leading priests to arrest everyone who calls upon your name." 15 But the Lord said, "Go, for Saul is my chosen instrument to take my message to the Gentiles and to kings, as well as to the people of Israel. 16 And I will show him how much he must suffer for my name's sake."

Acts 9:13-16

The story of Saul's conversion to Paul is thrilling. Saul was a man who was full of power and authority and he used that to bring havoc upon the church and the people of God. As he was doing this, as he was being a terrorist, the whole world of Christianity was being turned upside down. We wonder why God would use such a mean person in the ministry of the Lord. Well, Saul was converted. Have you ever thought why is the Lord using me or why he is using you? We were people at one point in life who were unconverted. He loved us anyway and loved us into the kingdom, so that should help us with our issues of being judgmental. You never can tell what the Lord's going to do to a person.

What did the Lord recognize in Saul that would make him useful in the kingdom? He was effective, he was efficient, he was obedient, he was loyal to the Sanhedrin, he was a good student, and he was task-driven; he sought to do whatever his assignment was to a degree of excellence. But he was wrong. He had the wrong information. He was going in the wrong

direction. Then he met Jesus on that Damascus Road and the light of Christ outshined the sun, like a solar eclipse, the Son of God was brighter than our own sun. The light of Christ struck Saul and he instantly cried out, Lord! This wasn't in reverence, but in submission to a power authority that was greater than he knew here on earth. Then the Lord interviewed him for his new assignment. He asked Saul, Why are you contrary to the church? Why are you kicking against me? That's a good point. The Lord said, why are you like someone taking a sharp stick and motivating an animal to move forward? Why have you decided to put your spurs on backwards so instead of hitting the animal, you're hurting yourself? The Lord wanted him to know that when you bother the least of these you have offended me. Isn't it wonderful to know that's what the Lord thinks of us?

> **The Lord wanted him to know that when you bother the least of these you have offended me. Isn't that wonderful to know that's what the Lord thinks of us?**

Well the story goes on that after this blinding episode of light, after this conversation in the middle of the desert at noontime, Saul got up and was taken, because he could no longer see, he was taken to a man's house. The man's name was Judas and he was called to be the host for this person who had a reputation of being a terrorist and a murderer. Judas opened his home to him. This is radical hospitality. Now, he might have been a little bit afraid. I know I would've been. Are you concerned about the type of people you take into your home or into your congregation? If God sends them, they are okay. If the Holy Spirit sends them to your door, they're okay. I'm sure Judas asked some questions, but God assured him in his spirit, Saul's okay, he's here to pray.

Then Ananias, another devout follower of Christ, was called to come and minister to this mean man named Saul. Ananias, the scripture records, did ask some questions. He said, What? You mean me? Talk to him? Now, Lord, you know what he's been doing. He's been killing and destroying the church and the people of God. You still want me to talk to him? The Lord said, Yes, I have chosen him to do a specific work. Out of obedience, Ananias went and prayed for Saul and instantly the power of the Holy Spirit came upon him. Now, it's not always instant in the Bible, but it was in this case and he was converted from Saul to Paul.

Let's think about these two men. Think about the hospitality of Judas, not Judas Iscariot — that was a different person. Think about the willingness and obedience of Ananias to do what the Lord asked him to do. Without those two instruments we wouldn't have this complete conversion story. They yielded to the will and call of God and now we have so many writings by Paul, so many words, so many stories about Paul that help us today in our ministry.

The Lord changed Saul's name. A lot of this had to do with his previous reputation being so bad that he needed a new name. The Lord changed his name so that the Christians, the followers of Christ, could have confidence in him. It was a long row for Paul to hoe though, he was not instantly accepted. The leaders in Jerusalem took pause, but the Lord had changed him.

Has your name been changed? Think about that. What did they used to call you when you were walking around in the community, when you were playing basketball, when you were a child, when you were an adolescent? What did they used to call you, and who are you today? Did they have a little nickname for you? Were you their little bad boy? Were you their little obnoxious girl? But look at you today. The Lord has converted you. The Lord has changed your name. And the Lord can use me and you, like Paul, to be very instrumental in bringing the light of Christ into the darkness of the lives of others. What did

the Lord do when he changed your name, when he changed your behavior, when he changed your direction, your path, your life? What is your conversion story?

Pastor Walter Henry Cross

God's Promises

Sweet Samples from Scripture

Pastor Walter Henry Cross

God's Way, Not Our Way

¹⁵ But the voice spoke again: "Do not call something unclean if God has made it clean."

Acts 10:15

In the tenth chapter of Acts, we read about Cornelius. Cornelius was a non-Jew and the Bible refers to him as a devout man, one of the devout brethren, some of the group of men and women who were of different historical heritage and embraced the teachings of Jesus Christ. He was one of those. And he desired the sincere milk of the word, not only for himself, but for his family and his friends. One day, the Lord gave him a vision. A celestial being showed up in his house and told him, gave him an assignment, to send some men with a message to the Apostle Peter. Cornelius could do that because he was a career military person and he had a certain number of men that he was in charge of, like a captain or a lieutenant. Since he was a man of a certain rank, he had the ability to dispatch these men to Peter. We remember Peter, the boisterous one who did all the talking. Now he's an established kingdom-builder but the Lord is continuing to work on him also. The angel told Cornelius, Send and get Peter and bring him to your house so he can teach you about the gospel concerning the freedom in Jesus Christ. Cornelius did.

At the same time, Peter was having a vision as well. He was praying. He was devout, he was involved in ministry, he was on the rooftop praying, he was not ashamed, and he was praying and beseeching the Lord. Now he had missed his mealtime. You

know it's not good for us to miss our mealtime and I try not to do that too often. But sometimes you get caught up in worship and praise and then you skip a meal in order to embrace the presence of the Lord. Well, Peter grew faint with the heat and with the lack of nourishment and he kind of went woozy and with that, he saw a vision of a sheet falling from heaven. It had all types of stuff on it, and he heard a voice that said, Rise, Peter, slay and eat, prepare, make your meal. Peter looked on that sheet that came down, held at the four and corners, and there were all kinds of creeping things, all kinds of flying things, all types of crawling things on it. He said, Oh Lord, no, this is not my tradition, this is not on my menu, this is not what historically I've been taught to eat, these things are unclean. And Peter got chastised immediately: Who are you to say that what I have created is unclean? Who are we to say that an individual God created is not worthy?

Peter had to learn that lesson. He didn't get it right then, because what he saw on that sheet did not whet his appetite. But the Lord also told him, There's two men coming to get you. I want you to go with them. They're not going to look like you, they're not going to be dressed like you, they're going to be visitors from afar, they're not going to be family members, they're not going to be your church members, they're not going to be your cousins, they're not going to belong to your fraternity, they're not going to be from your side of town, but they need you.

Now, notice that a lot of times, when the Lord is expressing to us to go, he does not feel obligated to tell us all the details. Remember Abraham? Remember Moses? He doesn't give us all the details, but he tells us to go. So, after this vision, this experience, this assignment, the men came. Peter went to the door and said, I knew you were coming, what do you want? They told him, Our captain, our lieutenant, our man, said come with us. And Peter said let me put a few little things in my backpack and get a couple of the fellows around here to go with

me and I'll go to Joppa with you. When he arrived at Cornelius' house, Cornelius was full of expectation. If you want the Lord to bless you, be full of expectation and faith. He went and got his family together. A man or a woman who loves the Lord always loves their family and wants their family to be safe. He got his family together and he went and got all his friends and loved ones, as many as he could. He probably had a sizeable house because he was a man of note and rank. He filled the house.

Well, Peter came in and he said, Now, you know, I'm not supposed to be here. This is not politically correct. I'm not being culturally sensitive. But the Lord said. Think about that a minute, *but the Lord said.* I know we are driven by this prevailing culture, and there are some places we don't go, some people we don't talk to, some situations we just don't have an appetite for, but remember what Peter said. But the Lord said for Peter to go to Cornelius' house and Peter did. He went there and preached the word of God and the place became filled with the power of the Holy Spirit and baptisms took place. And Peter summarized this for us. I don't even have to do a summary, he did. He said, Lord, now I know what you were talking about when you let that sheet down. You were telling me not to have any partiality, don't pick and choose who should be saved, don't pick and choose who should belong to the church, don't pick and choose whose house I can visit and knock on and present the gospel.

I was telling someone earlier that if there was only chocolate ice cream, that'd be best ice cream in the world, but Baskin-Robbins has 31 flavors. That causes me a sense of confusion and sometimes I test two or three before I get to my decision. That's not what the Lord wants us to do. He doesn't want us to pick and choose, to test out, he wants us to be devoted first. Let's define that. Cornelius prayed, he had a prayer relationship, he had a continuous conversation. That's the key word, conversation. He wasn't telling God what to do. He had a continuous conversation. That means he listened to God as

well as made his petitions known. He worshiped and celebrated God's presence. That's all part of a prayer life. And then he was a good steward. He was generous. These two things are necessary if you're going to be a devout person, generosity and having a close relationship with the Lord by keeping your prayer life in order. Then the Lord will use you.

Think about Peter's statement about being impartial. Has there been a time when the Lord tugged at your heart to do something and you said, Lord, you know I don't fool with those people? Sometimes we say that about our own family. We tell the Lord, You know I went over to my cousin's house last Thanksgiving and my cousin did this and that, and I'm not going to go back. But God calls us to those places that we don't naturally want to go or to situations we don't naturally see ourselves involved in. God is telling us not to treat humanity like the drive-thru McDonald's, where we can look at the menu and pick and choose, where we can squeeze old Ronald's nose and pick and choose what we're going to have and how we're going to have it. Then there's another company that says, We'll fix it your way. The Lord is telling Peter, Cornelius, and me and you that it's not going to be our way, it's going to be his way. We need to rejoice about that. Has God ever convicted you of trying to do something your way?

Pastor Walter Henry Cross

Don't Play With Fire

¹² Then God said, "I am giving you a sign of my covenant with you and with all living creatures, for all generations to come. ¹³ I have placed my rainbow in the clouds. It is the sign of my covenant with you and with all the earth. ¹⁴ When I send clouds over the earth, the rainbow will appear in the clouds, ¹⁵ and I will remember my covenant with you and with all living creatures. Never again will the floodwaters destroy all life. ¹⁶ When I see the rainbow in the clouds, I will remember the eternal covenant between God and every living creature on earth." ¹⁷ Then God said to Noah, "Yes, this rainbow is the sign of the covenant I am confirming with all the creatures on earth."

Genesis 9:12-17

A covenant is an agreement, a contractual agreement in modern language, an agreement between two parties. It's an understanding and it's more vital than just an acknowledgment that I'm going to do this if you do that. When God speaks of covenant, he has no other person, no other entity, no other situation that God needs to verify himself with, his word is good enough for a covenant, for a promise. God made a promise to a man called Noah. We're very familiar with Noah's story. Noah was given an assignment from God to assemble people on a large barge-like boat that we call an ark. Noah and his family and reproductive animals of all kinds were to be put on the boat. This was a very intense project that God gave him. He had to gather all the animals; God called them so that they knew where to go. Noah had to get the right food, whatever's

necessary to preserve life during this time of devastation and flood.

God did a reset of the world. The world had gotten so bad, so wicked, so indifferent to God, so perverse, so twisted that God did a reset. Now had God make a mistake so that he had to pull his eraser out and change things? No, God didn't make a mistake. He made the world and the people and the animals perfect but man, given choice, mankind, humankind, through Adam and Eve, given choice, chose to walk away from the will and the word of God, and to enter sin. Sin became pervasive and God did a reset. That reset was mercy. Now when my teachers were giving my papers back and had written all over in red at the top indicating that they were going to give me an opportunity to do the work all over again, that was grace. That was not a failing grade. I needed to receive it and accept it as an opportunity to do better. God's given humankind an opportunity to do better.

So, the flood has happened and it's all over and Noah comes out of the boat. I'm sure he's getting relief. He's been dealing with animals and all of the kind of stuff that animals have for us to deal with. If you've ever had a pet, ever had a horse, ever raised animals, you know that animals in a close confined area would be very interesting for a prolonged period of time. So, I can see him coming out of the boat with a little degree of relief. He's been feeding and taking care of everything, he's been doing what God told him to do. There's always a blessing ahead of us when we do what God tells us to do.

God speaks to Noah and tells him the flood is over. The world has been reset. The animals were going out to reproduce and to flourish throughout the world. Noah's family is going to have an opportunity to live and thrive in this new, cleansed world. God says, I want to make a promise. I want to make a covenant between me and you, that I'm not going to destroy this world with flood waters again and I'm going to give you this covenant as a gift. Often when people give me a gift, they take the time

to wrap it up and put a little bow on it, they don't just hand it to me. They fix it up and I have the joy of unwrapping it. God put a bow on this covenant. He put a rainbow in the heavens, a colorful, beautiful sign of God's lasting love, grace, and mercy toward humankind.

Now, in my heritage, they used to sing a little kids song and they sang, no more water, but fire next time. Don't we know, even now, the leaders of this world are playing with fire? They have taken fire to their bosom, they're playing with ballistic fire, with words of fire, with actions of fire, with the evil of fire. This scripture could be prophetically applied to us today. God has promised no more annihilation. But he did not promise that he would not do another reset. God said there will be life among humankind and animal kind. Isn't it interesting that importance was placed upon the animal kingdom? I think we should take that to heart. All of God's creation is vital and very important. I think we should take that to heart. God took the time to tell Noah that the animals were important also.

So, we have a biblical promise that there will not be total annihilation of the earth again. But we also have a promise that God is just. That should give us pause and opportunity for prayer. We need to pray for our world leaders, the ones we agree with as well as the ones we don't agree with. Take note also that we are playing with fire in our own lives when we walk away from what God has given us in the Bible as a code of life, as a code of ethics, and respect for all kinds of life. What can we do as individuals to lay down our fire and pick up the love of God? How can we lay down our destructive fire, our mean-spirited fire, our separating fire, our ballistic fire? What can each of us do as an individual? I know you don't control the world, but you have a whole lot to do with you.

Sweet Samples from Scripture

Pastor Walter Henry Cross

Marked by God's Promise

³ At this, Abram fell face down on the ground. Then God said to him, ⁴ "This is my covenant with you: I will make you the father of a multitude of nations! ⁵ What's more, I am changing your name. It will no longer be Abram. Instead, you will be called Abraham, for you will be the father of many nations. ⁶ I will make you extremely fruitful. Your descendants will become many nations, and kings will be among them! ⁷ "I will confirm my covenant with you and your descendants after you, from generation to generation. This is the everlasting covenant: I will always be your God and the God of your descendants after you. ⁸ And I will give the entire land of Canaan, where you now live as a foreigner, to you and your descendants. It will be their possession forever, and I will be their God." ⁹ Then God said to Abraham, "Your responsibility is to obey the terms of the covenant. You and all your descendants have this continual responsibility. ¹⁰ This is the covenant that you and your descendants must keep: Each male among you must be circumcised.

¹³ All must be circumcised. Your bodies will bear the mark of my everlasting covenant.

Genesis 17:3-10, 13

Being a Sunday school scholar, you know that the names of Abram and Sarai were changed later on to Abraham and Sarah. And we understand that so often in the Bible when names have been changed, they were changed according to the destiny that God had for that person. A lot of times our names are changed because God wants us to walk into a certain pre-planned destiny that he has for us. No, our birth certificates

are still the same, but what people call us is different. They may have called us lazy and now we're ambitious. They may have called us lackadaisical and now we're head-starters. They may have called us sinners and now we're sinners in the process of being saved. They may have called us bad and now we're looking for every way possible to be empowered by the presence of the Holy Spirit to live according to the will of the Lord. They don't call us what they used to because our name has been written down in glory and I'm glad.

Abram and Sarai were selected by God to be the head or the beginning of a mighty nation, the nation of Israel. God called them to this. He gave them that assignment and talked to them person to person. They were a little skeptical because they were up in age. They were octogenarians, they were in their 80s and 90s and they thought, well, how can this thing be? You've heard that before. And you've probably thought that about some of the assignments that God has given you, how could this thing possibly be? If God said it, it can be done.

Well, a period of time passed since the initiation of the idea into the hearts and minds of Abram and Sarai and nothing happened. As we often do, they decided to take matters into their own hands. Sarai came up with an idea that would circumvent or help out the Lord's plan. How many of us know that there's nothing I can do to help God out? All I need to do is say yes. That is what obedience and faith is all about. Well in the due course of time, what happened? They had made a huge mistake and another child was born, not the one promised by God, but through the handmaid of Sarah. That caused confusion that is still existent in the world today.

Well, the right time came, and God sent the son of promise. He sent the son that would be in the lineage of the entire nation of the Jews. Now God had repeated, reiterated, and said again in his covenant promise that he was going to make Abram the father of a great nation. Abram means wonderful or glorious or honored father. Abraham means father of many. God did not

take away from Abram's name, he just added on to it. Abraham was going to be a wonderful, glorious, honorable father, but now of many. So many that they could not even be numbered.

At this point, God decided to seal his covenant promise. We've talked before about a covenant, a contractual agreement between two or more people, also between man and God, a promise. What has God promised us? He promised Abraham that he would be over this mighty nation, that he would be the source of all of it, and God sealed this in blood. This is where the idea of circumcision comes in. Circumcision pre-existed the time of Abraham. Other countries and other tribes used this ritual and had different applications for its meaning. This time the meaning was that God said, I want to put a mark on man, that man will remember my promise. Remember the rainbow, a promise-keeping symbol? This is another promise-keeping symbol. Circumcision is the surgical removal of the foreskin on the reproductive organ of the male child. And Abraham had to go through this process when he was 99 years old, along with his son. Ever since that time, most Orthodox Jews have continued this practice. Other people, who are not Jewish, do the same practice for different reasons. Some do it for religious reasons, some for personal hygiene. In this case it was a symbol for making a mark, just like you might mark right here, check right here, or put your X here. Many of these individuals would become soldiers on the field. They could be identified in case of disaster or warfare. They could be identified because God put a mark on them.

Now, my brothers and sisters, there have been times when you've been in the restaurant, you've been in grocery store, you've been in the hospital and somebody walks up to you and says, I want you to pray for me, I felt led to talk to you. Why is that? God has put a mark on you and no, not a knife or a sharpened flint stone has come to touch your body. But God Almighty has put a mark on you to assure even unbelievers that you belong to him. Think of a time in your life when you

have not said to anyone that you were a believer or even that you attended church, but people have invested confidence in you because they believed that you were a person in tune to Almighty God. That's the mark of the covenant. That's the mark of the promise. One of the promises God has made to us is eternal life. We have opportunity, through Jesus Christ and his sacrifice, to live in heaven with God the Father forever. That promise also has a token, it has a signature, it has the symbol of blood in Calvary at the execution of Jesus Christ, plus the resurrection. God has signed his name in blood. He's given us another opportunity to know beyond a shadow of a doubt that he is a promise keeper.

Pastor Walter Henry Cross

Holy Rest

⁸ "Remember to observe the Sabbath day by keeping it holy. ⁹ You have six days each week for your ordinary work, ¹⁰ but the seventh day is a Sabbath day of rest dedicated to the Lord your God. On that day no one in your household may do any work. This includes you, your sons and daughters, your male and female servants, your livestock, and any foreigners living among you. ¹¹ For in six days the Lord made the heavens, the earth, the sea, and everything in them; but on the seventh day he rested. That is why the Lord blessed the Sabbath day and set it apart as holy.

Exodus 20:8-11

God always keeps his promise. We've been talking about signs or symbols of God's promise, God's signature. He signed his name in blood through circumcision. He gave us his package of love through the rainbow. Sabbath rest is another of God's promises to us and an agreement that we need to uphold. God will take care of us and God will be with us, but God deserves honor and worship and we need rest. My brothers and sisters, some of you are multitaskers and you do real good at it. I wish I could do that. I endeavor to do one thing well. My hat goes off to all of you, especially the ladies, because you're very good at doing multiple things at the same time. What I want to encourage all of us to do is to remember Sabbath rest. It is a holy thing. It is the time that we take to be alone with God in reverence.

Pastors, Sabbath rest is not Sunday for you because we work on Sunday. We need to find time during the week to

observe Sabbath rest. If someone comes by and tells you, whether you are a teacher, a pastor, or a student, that you are workaholic, it's not a compliment. That's not God's will for you. I understand that there are certain budget requirements that come along in life and your pattern of work may change but try to get back to the observance of holy rest. It's sacred.

> **If someone comes by and tells you, whether you are a teacher, a pastor, or a student, that you are workaholic, it's not a compliment. That's not God's will for you.**

This discussion about Sabbath is not about the calendar or what day of the week we should worship, it's about making time to be alone with the Lord. We need to cultivate time for us to rest. If somebody is telling you that you're working yourself to death, again, that is not a compliment. You're not being wise, you're not being prudent, you're not being a good steward of the body, the mind, and the soul the Lord has given you.

There are very subtle things, especially in the church, where people will encourage you to go beyond where God is requiring you to go. You may be told, well, brother or sister, you do that so well, you need to do it all the time. But I'm telling you, brothers and sisters in leadership, and remember, everybody in the church is a potential leader, you always should be working yourself out of a job. Every time you get in a position of leadership, you should be developing someone else to walk along with you so that, at some point in time, you can turn that work over. Don't work yourself to death. That's spiritual and physical suicide and that's not of God.

You may say, well, preacher if I don't do it, it won't get done. I used to say that. Some of the churches I used to serve, I used to wonder how they were going to make it without me. But they did just fine, because I was not God in their lives. God was all

they needed. God had me there for a season and for a reason. And if I would observe holy Sabbath rest, I would understand that God is the one who's really in charge.

We need to make opportunities that we can use to refresh, reflect, renew, and recreate ourselves. You're going to be a better husband if you take Sabbath rest. You're going to be a better father, you're going to be a better mother, you're going to be a better friend, you're going to be a better kingdom-worker if you take the time and follow the principles in Exodus 20 and employ, observe, and honor Sabbath rest in your life. If you're a choir member and you're singing on Sunday, in two or three different services, find time during the week to sing to yourself.

What are some opportunities where you can squeeze out some Sabbath rest? It could be walking in the mall, not shopping, just walking in the mall. It could be walking in the park or walking alongside the river. The time is not nearly as important as the activity of being alone with God. It can be a sacred five minutes or eight hours or twenty-four hours. Christian believers, it is necessary, if you want to be fully utilized by the power of Christ in your life, to observe Sabbath rest. Figure out a way to rest. Be honest. If you feel driven all the time, is that the power of the Holy Spirit or is that your ego driving you? If you don't do it, God can.

Sweet Samples from Scripture

Pastor Walter Henry Cross

Covenant Lessons

Sweet Samples from Scripture

Spiritual Heart Surgery

22 "Therefore, give the people of Israel this message from the Sovereign Lord: I am bringing you back, but not because you deserve it. I am doing it to protect my holy name, on which you brought shame while you were scattered among the nations. 23 I will show how holy my great name is—the name on which you brought shame among the nations. And when I reveal my holiness through you before their very eyes, says the Sovereign Lord, then the nations will know that I am the Lord. 24 For I will gather you up from all the nations and bring you home again to your land. 25 "Then I will sprinkle clean water on you, and you will be clean. Your filth will be washed away, and you will no longer worship idols. 26 And I will give you a new heart, and I will put a new spirit in you. I will take out your stony, stubborn heart and give you a tender, responsive heart. 27 And I will put my Spirit in you so that you will follow my decrees and be careful to obey my regulations.

Ezekiel 36:22-27

Let's talk about about another symbol or sign or token of Covenant. This time, the token, the symbol, is the heart of man. In the book of Ezekiel, the nation of Israel finds themselves in captivity and we know the reason why. It's sin. It is their consistent, habitual addiction to idolatry. Anything that we put in front of our Lord and Savior Jesus Christ, whatever we worship that's not our one and only and holy God, is idolatry. They didn't get it. We have a hard time getting it sometimes. They didn't get it at all. Think of the see-saw that goes up and down. They would go into captivity, they would

be repentant, they would be restored, they would be delivered, and then they'd start the whole process over again. Then along would come another prophet telling them the warning of the Lord. The Lord was very patient with Israel. The Lord is very patient with us today. We have some of those same tendencies to follow after whatever is going on in the culture that pleases our fleshly appetites.

The Lord was very patient with Israel. The Lord is very patient with us today.

To zero in on what these Ezekiel is talking about this morning, the nation of Israel has been taken captive and the important and talented men and women and boys and girls have been taken off. The captors have plundered their homeland and go back and forth through the broken walls of the city of Jerusalem and take the people from Israel to this foreign land. When the captives get there, something interesting happens. The people of Israel, the captives, become assimilated to the prevailing culture. Isn't that interesting? It's like the church becoming like the world, do you know anything about that? It's like me and you being all religious and righteous on Sunday morning but not distinguishable as a Christian during the week, as if we have no spiritual identity except when we're in the worship mode or in the worship setting. God doesn't like this. In fact, God has a word for that. He said that we are, I'm including you and myself, profaning the name of God. You are making God look bad, I am making God look bad when I say hallelujah, praise the Lord, and then go out and live any kind of way and embrace idolatry in this world. Or when I think that I must scratch where I itch without being reverent and without making choices that would lift up our Heavenly Father in glory.

Let me tell you where God started with the people in this text. They were in captivity, and the Lord said, I'm going to

do something because the people who have captured you are looking at God Jehovah in a curious way. The captors were wondering, why would your God, who you love so much and who you say is over all and is the only true God, why would he kick you out of your own land? God tells his people, through Ezekiel, you have marred my name. This is what has happened, you have gone off to this foreign country, unto punishment in captivity, and you have taken on their traits, you have taken on their gods, and you have made my name look bad among the heathens. Heathens in this case means unbelievers. Are we doing this? Are we living in such a way that we make the God that we serve look bad? Are we crucifying the flesh of Christ anew? Think about it, think about it.

So, where did God start? He said I'm going to do something about this. What he decided to do was to bring about revival in the land. With the crops, with the fields, with the animals, he was going to give his captive people a sense of prosperity, but not because they deserved it. He started with the heart. He said, I'm going to take that old fickle, addictive, abusive, mean-spirited, ornery, ugly-acting, stone-cold heart out and give you a heart that's pumping love, a heart of flesh. This was a heart matter.

Now, my brothers and sisters, you can change your clothes but you're not going to live right until you change your heart. You can change your song, change your address, get yourself a new car, I don't care what you change, but there's no change unless there's a heart change, unless you allow the power of God to do spiritual surgery. The heart in this case means the seat of all our reasoning and thinking, it's what we really are. I'm not talking about the organ that's pumping blood, I'm talking about your mind, the way you think, the way you think when you don't know anyone else is listening to your motives.

God has blessed us when we really didn't deserve it. We're blessed this morning. All we need to do is say, thank you Jesus. But we're not blessed because we're so good, we're not blessed

because we're so kind. We are blessed because God made a decision, a choice, to bless us, and we need to say thank you right there. Think about that moment that you received a heart change. And if your heart is not beating in tune with the Word of God, stop and pray, Lord, give me a clean heart, give me a new heart, allow me to be in step and in tune with you, because I don't want to live in such a way to take away from the name of God Jehovah. Lord, allow me to be a blessing.

Pastor Walter Henry Cross

Are You Hindering God?

² But Abram replied, "O Sovereign Lord, what good are all your blessings when I don't even have a son? Since you've given me no children, Eliezer of Damascus, a servant in my household, will inherit all my wealth. ³ You have given me no descendants of my own, so one of my servants will be my heir." ⁴ Then the Lord said to him, "No, your servant will not be your heir, for you will have a son of your own who will be your heir." ⁵ Then the Lord took Abram outside and said to him, "Look up into the sky and count the stars if you can. That's how many descendants you will have!"

Genesis 15:2-5

We've been talking about covenant and about some of the symbols, the tokens, the signs, of covenant that God has put out there so that we can understand that he has made an agreement with us and for us. We need to talk about the nature of God at this point. God is not like an attorney or a legal aid person. God is not like a notary public when you sign these agreements at the real estate office or at the bank or at the car dealership. God does not need our compliance. It would be good for us to comply, but God is all-sufficient. God makes the agreement; he does not have to validate himself with any other entity because there's not another entity that is necessary for God to keep his promise. We need witnesses and we need collateral, we need all of that stuff and then sometimes we still default on our contractual agreements. But with this covenant with God, he will not and cannot default. Based on that reality, we need to trust him, and we need to go with that agreement.

God had made an agreement, a covenant with Abram that he would be the father of a mighty nation. There was this period of time that Abram had to wait for the fulfillment of the promise and, to him, using his human time, his Timex or his Apple watch or whatever he was using, it didn't look like it was going to happen. He kept looking at the calendar and looking up at God, looking at the calendar and looking up at God — don't we do that? We realize the biblical promises that God has made to us and then we want to put God on a time schedule. But, as Romans says, May it never be. It's all in God's good time.

Now here is an opportunity. Our brother Abram is frustrated. God, you told me, but I don't have a son. You told me I was going to be a father of many, but I'm not even the father of one. Show me something, do something. Then we see that the Lord answers his prayer of desperation and comes into the situation to show him, in a deep sleep, the reality of the fact that God always keeps his promises. There was this division of animals, they cut them in half, a sacrifice. It was a bloody scene, but God often uses blood to testify of his truthfulness in covenant. The animals were separated and then God came down in the symbol of a fire pot with smoke going up to heaven, like incense represents prayers going up, and God made the promise between himself and himself. We call it the Abrahamic covenant, but God made that promise with himself, because there's not a man or a heavenly entity that has the capability of verifying anything for God. God is God all by himself.

Trust me. God said it, and if God said it, he surely will do it.

What can we glean from this? We need to trust God. But I don't see a little bouncing baby boy on my knee. Abram, look up, the Lord told him. Look into the heavens, see all those stars up there. Can you count them? Of course he couldn't count them.

In that day, before air pollution and smokestacks and tailpipes, you could look into the heavens and see millions and billions and trillions of stars. And the Lord said to him, your legacy, your heritage, your family, your seed, will be more numerous than these stars that you can't even count. Trust me. God said it, and if God said it, he surely will do it. My brothers and sisters, boys and girls, we need to change the way we think in terms of God's covenant promises toward us. If God has promised through his word that he's going to provide, that he's going to be there to protect, that he's going to multiply, that he's going to bless, we need to trust that. We need to come into agreement with God. God has already agreed with us, I am your Father and I fail not. I am the one who brought you into existence, I can handle this.

> **If God has promised through his word that he's going to provide, that he's going to be there to protect, that he's going to multiply, that he's going to bless, we need to trust that.**

Well, we remember that Abram and his wife decided to help God. Believe me, God does not need my help. I've tried that before and it didn't work out well. We need to wait. The Bible says that those who wait on the Lord shall renew their strength. We are depleted of strength today because we decide to go ahead and push the envelope toward God. God is not one we need to negotiate with. He's not one we need to play Let's Make a Deal with. We need to accept his covenant agreement and let him do it. We hinder God through disbelief. We hinder God through lack of faith. We put a limitation on God because we like to interject what we think and what we believe ought to have been done, what we would have done.

Now, I know we have no power to actually hinder God, but what I mean is that we live beneath our privileges, because God is ready and willing and equipped to bless us. A lot of times we move out of the stream, the flow of blessedness, because we get like Abram. That's why this story is in the Bible. It's to let us know, when we cannot see what God is doing, trust him. When we cannot tell at all what God is doing, to trust him. We don't know what God is doing behind the scenes, but guess what? Whatever God is doing, it's going to work out fine. What have you done to agree with God? Remember, God's already in agreement with me and you. As you ponder these things, you may be thinking, maybe I am in God's way, maybe I do need to let go and let God. God's not subject to our power, he has all power. We need to receive with faith his covenant agreement.

Pastor Walter Henry Cross

Be Prepared

¹⁰ Then the Lord told Moses, "Go down and prepare the people for my arrival. Consecrate them today and tomorrow, and have them wash their clothing. ¹¹ Be sure they are ready on the third day, for on that day the Lord will come down on Mount Sinai as all the people watch.

Exodus 19:10-11

In Exodus 19, we see a very interesting scene. The history has been rehearsed about the Lord delivering the children of Israel from captivity in the land of Egypt. Now they're on their way. The Lord has provided them everything that they need in terms of food and clothes that didn't wear out. They didn't have to go to the dry cleaners or to a laundromat. God provided and that shows God's love. You know that he's still providing for me and you to this very moment? We're sitting here today only because the Lord is providing.

Now let's look a little farther. We see this scene of a mountain in convulsion. A volcano is the closest we can come to describing it and sitting on top of this mountain is a thunderstorm, a cloud of lightning and fire and smoke. The Lord God Almighty has arrived. The people at one time thought that they wanted to talk to God for themselves, they hadn't wanted any pastor, any shepherd, any prophet, they wanted to cut out the middleman. They said, You call God, tell him to come down here and we'll talk with him. Well, after God put on this display of his power and his majesty, they said, No, Moses, you go ahead, we'll be right here when you get back.

So, we see Moses interacting with God at the top of Mount Sinai, which was being set on fire by the power of God. God calls Moses up, gives Moses instructions: tell the people not to touch the mountain and put a border around the mountain, don't let them follow you. He said this because the human experience is inquisitive, or as my grandmother would say, just plain nosy. God said, They don't need to come up here and view what you're seeing, this is for you. Later on, the Lord allows him to bring Aaron, his assistant, his executive administrator. He lets Aaron come up and view what's going on in this communication between man and God. God tells Moses, I'm going to give you my word. You take my word to my people.

One of the things that we get out of this is order. God deserves order. This is the Old Testament, this is the former dispensation, you'll hear theologians and preachers say. But Jesus did not erase the Old Testament, he enhanced the Old Testament. There is still order in leadership, there is still order in the way God wants things done. Now Jesus is our go-to person. He gives us the privilege and the honor to approach the holy throne of God through his blood sacrifice and suffering. We need to keep that order in mind. When I end my prayer, and I'm not suggesting that you have to do this but it's my personal order, I say, In the name of Jesus, in the name of Jesus the Christ we ask these things, amen. That's one way that order in my life helps to keep me grounded as I approach this mountain of privilege, this mountain of fire. The Word of God that was etched on those tablets is not in the waste-disposal can. God still hates murder, God still hates sin, but we have an opportunity to eradicate sin in our human experience by our relationship and belief in Jesus Christ.

There's a troubling word in this set of scriptures. First of all it says, people sanctify yourself, consecrate yourself, take a bath, put on your Sunday go-to-meeting clothes. It's very important to note what the Lord is saying. Prepare yourself, get ready for worship. Worship is so important. Everybody who

knows me knows this, worship must be anticipated. Choir directors, don't just get up and fan your hands on Sunday morning, be prepared. Organist, pianist, be prepared. Rehearse. Don't let that be the first time you play that music. Preachers and teachers, don't get up and run your finger down on the scripture saying, So what we're going to do this morning is wait on the Holy Spirit. Wait all week. God is so worthy. Be prepared on Sunday morning. But then the verse says to not touch a woman. What is that all about?

God is saying that, in terms of order, worshiping him and honoring him precedes human relationships. Now we've got soccer on Sunday morning, I don't fight soccer. We've got softball, we've got a band trip, we've got camping, we've got fly fishing, all on Sunday morning, and I won't even get to the football. Worship. The Lord said put me, God Almighty, ahead of human relationships. Nothing will be denied. God is not telling you not to do all of these wonderful things, but he is saying, Put me first. I am a God of order and for you to receive my word, you must be ready. The process of covenant is to be ready. You don't sign an agreement unless you're ready to own, insure, and drive a car with a license. You don't sign a contract for a new house unless you are ready to occupy it, have the ceiling patched, make sure the windows are ready. If you sign that contract and you're not ready, you're not going to be there long. Get ready. Be ready. God has signed in blood his agreement. Agree with God to prepare your life, to prepare your vessel to be inhabited by the presence of Almighty God.

Sweet Samples from Scripture

Pastor Walter Henry Cross

Covenant Obedience

³ Then Moses went down to the people and repeated all the instructions and regulations the Lord had given him. All the people answered with one voice, "We will do everything the Lord has commanded."

Exodus 24:3

Let's talk about obedience. God gave the law to Moses on that fiery mountain for the people to obey. We've spent a lot of time in our lives rehearsing and memorizing and saying the Ten Commandments, and they still are the Ten Commandments. When Jesus summarized the law as love toward heaven, the Father, and love toward each other, he did not erase the law. He embraced it and enhanced it. We need to remember that. We're not exempt from doing the right thing. We're certainly not exempt from our covenant relationship with God the Father. We're not exempt from obedience.

We have talked before about order. We talked about order in worship and order in leadership. The law brings order to the hearts and minds of men and women, boys and girls. The commandments are examples of the core values that God requires of his people. God wants us to be and to act a certain way. To do that, we must be obedient to what the Lord has said. The Lord has kept his agreement. He has allowed the very begotten Son of God to come down and die and remove sin's stain from our lives if we would only believe. That's what God has done. He has kept his covenant agreement. Now, will we obey?

The children of Israel saw the demonstration of fire and power and the majesty of Almighty God. Then, Moses came back down from the mountain and his face was shining and the smoke was still around. So, the people stepped back from the mountain and they said to Moses, Whatever God told you to tell us, we're going to do it. Now, we know it didn't last long, but that brings us to what are we going to do? We have promised God in covenant agreement so many times. Lord bless me, and he did; Lord save me, and he has; Lord increase, and he keeps on blessing us. He has stayed the hand of the enemy. Now the question is, are we obedient? Are we doing what the Lord said?

We need to know the Word of God because we believe that there's life there.

The first thing we need to do if we're going to be obedient is to be students of the word. We need to know what the Lord is asking us to do. We need to know what our assignment is. We need to study the word as a lifestyle, not just for Sunday school class, not just to help us fall asleep at night, but we need to study the Word of God as a lifestyle. Have you ever seen some young people with their telephone, how they study that phone as part of their lifestyle? They can text without looking. They know how to go into the network, into the menu, and how to bring up different things. That's all good. They've helped me with mine. But they have studied it, they know it. We need to know the Word of God because we believe that there's life there. After we have acquired and are still acquiring knowledge, we need to do what the word says. We need to practice. As part of our covenant relationship with God Almighty, we need to practice obedience. If the Lord said it, we need to endeavor to do it.

What's so wonderful about this covenant? The Lord has not left us without assistance. We have the power and the presence of the Holy Spirit with us to enable us to obey the Word of God.

Now if your conscience is seared, you do whatever you want to do, whatever you think you're big and bad enough to do, and then you sleep well at night. That's a dangerous position, my brothers and sisters. That's not a good place to be. I would suggest that we pray for increased sensitivity to the Word of God and increased awareness of determining what God is saying to us. Then we need to find ourselves doing the will of God based upon his word and living within his way.

I want you to think about ways that we can be more obedient to the Word of God. Remember, number one is we have to know it. Number two is we need to follow it; we need to do it. There's a blessing waiting for you at the other end of obedience. Now if you make a mistake, don't wallow in your error. Fall forward. Get up, ask for forgiveness, for renewal through the washing, cleansing, purging blood of Jesus, and start out again. Obey the word of God.

Sweet Samples from Scripture

Pastor Walter Henry Cross

A Covenant With David

¹ When King David was settled in his palace and the Lord had given him rest from all the surrounding enemies, ² the king summoned Nathan the prophet. "Look," David said, "I am living in a beautiful cedar palace, but the Ark of God is out there in a tent!" ³ Nathan replied to the king, "Go ahead and do whatever you have in mind, for the Lord is with you." ⁴ But that same night the Lord said to Nathan, ⁵ "Go and tell my servant David, 'This is what the Lord has declared: Are you the one to build a house for me to live in?

2nd Samuel 7:1-5

God's covenant promise to David in 2nd Samuel is often referred to as the Davidic covenant. Now as we open this chapter, let's see what's going on. First of all, we see David in a time of peace. He was a warrior and God had been with him through many battles. He's been victorious and now there's a season of peace in the land among God's people. David has taken this opportunity to come and build these magnificent palaces and official buildings for the nation and for his own personal residence. And on this particular day there might have been a moment of guilt or it might have been just a feeling that I've done all this for me, what have I done for the Lord? Have you had that thought lately? That's a good thought.

Well, David called Nathan, or Nathan happened to be by. Nathan was a prophet, a man of God, and Nathan was very instrumental in the life of the king and the king's government. It's interesting that often times in high official places in the Word of God, we see a man of God or a woman of God very

present in the decision-making process. That would be very helpful today if our decision-making processes on the local level, the national level, and around the world included consulting with a person who is in a relationship with the Lord. When David expressed his desire to do something for the Lord, out of thanksgiving and out of worship and out of honor, Nathan said for him to go forward. The prophet said, You've done well in battle and you're prosperous and the things you touch have been very good, so go forward.

That night, after they finished their power lunch or whatever they had, the Lord God Almighty spoke to Nathan. He said, Go back to the king and tell him this. I haven't been in a residence of permanency since we left Egypt. I have been dwelling in the tents and I have not summoned anybody, any prophet, any king, or any leader to tell them to build me a house. I think, people of God, it'd be wise if we waited until God tells us to build a house. There are so many houses of worship today that are choking the people because of debt. If you're struggling this morning to pay for a house, it could be that God did not tell you to build it. At least not then, at least not there, and maybe not at all.

But David had a good desire, he had a vision. The Lord did not chastise him for his vision. Instead, the Lord said, Let me offer you something different; I want to build you a house. David was overwhelmed with joy. He said to God, You've been so good to me, you've been so kind to the people of Israel and I wanted to build you a house. Now you tell me you're going to build me a house? Then God told him, No, not so many square feet, not a vaulted ceiling, not ivory columns, not dual appointments. No this is going to be a spiritual house, a legacy, a dynasty. I'm going to allow your son, Solomon, to build the house. Solomon represents a time of peace in the nation of Israel. He can be referred to as the king of peace. Now, he didn't do everything right. Kind of like me and you, he didn't do everything right but during his reign there was a time of prolonged peace.

Now there's a prophecy here that we need to take special look at. This is a twofold prophecy or parallel prophecy. The son of King David was to build the house of God. Here were some of the instructions. If he disobeys me, the Lord said, I will punish him but his throne, his legacy, his family, which is genetically related to you, King David, will go on forever. We have two ideas that we need to flesh out here. The prophecy was referring to King Solomon, the son of David. The prophecy was also referring to Jesus Christ the Messiah. His throne is the one that will rule all and continue forever. We have other verses to back that up. If you have time, look at Psalm 89. If you make time to read that, you'll see a summary of the covenant in chapter 7 of 2nd Samuel. The Lord said, The house of the Lord that I'm going to build for you, David, is not going to have any fine appointments that will rot and decay. You won't have to rip the carpet up or change the air conditioner, you won't have to do any of that stuff. But this house will rule forever. It's going to come through the lineage of Jesse and through the family of David. What did they call Jesus? The son of David. So, in this chapter you see he, being the son of David in the natural sense, his son Solomon, and he again, in the spiritual sense, the Son of David that is our Lord and Savior Jesus Christ.

We need to listen to what God is saying. A lot of times we have some great ideas, but our covenant father, our covenant guardian, would have us to wait on him before we launch out. If you have a church that seats 250 people, then it can hold a thousand people on the weekend with a Saturday night service and services on Sunday morning, at midday, and then again Sunday night. If you have a thousand people attending worship, you can do it in a 250-seat auditorium over the weekend before you break ground for a new mega church. Listen to God. How many scholarships could we pay with that kind of money? Listen to God. How many meals could we feed, and not just at Thanksgiving and Christmas? We could do it all year-round if we listen to God.

David wanted to do a good thing. God celebrated that with him, but he wanted to do a better thing that was to usher in the kingdom of Jesus Christ. I want you to think of things that turned out better because you paused to wait on God. Even though what you had planned to do was not necessarily a bad thing, but when you waited on God it turned out differently. And then, let's be honest. Let's think about the things that we didn't consult the Lord about. Things that we made up our mind about over lunch or woke up one morning with a bright idea, then we went ahead and didn't consult God. How did it turn out?

Pastor Walter Henry Cross

Signing Up Again

² So on October 8 Ezra the priest brought the Book of the Law before the assembly, which included the men and women and all the children old enough to understand. ³ He faced the square just inside the Water Gate from early morning until noon and read aloud to everyone who could understand. All the people listened closely to the Book of the Law.

⁵ Ezra stood on the platform in full view of all the people. When they saw him open the book, they all rose to their feet. ⁶ Then Ezra praised the Lord, the great God, and all the people chanted, "Amen! Amen!" as they lifted their hands. Then they bowed down and worshiped the Lord with their faces to the ground.

Nehemiah 8:2-3, 5-6

We have another covenant lesson in Nehemiah. Nehemiah was a man who was given an assignment by God. His assignment was to fortify the city of Jerusalem. Now, as we remember our Biblical history, Jerusalem had been destroyed. There were certain kings who permitted some of the exiles, over a period of time, to return and begin the process of rebuilding the city. There were individuals who did not go into exile and were still in the area of Jerusalem, and they needed to know the story of their heritage. The writer of the book of Nehemiah depicts the story being told by the elders to the younger ones. We need to preserve our legacy as well by telling our story. We need to tell it over. We need to tell it in creative ways, and we need to tell it often. We need to let our young people know, let our new generations know of what the Lord has done in our heritage as Christians.

No matter what your family legacy might be, you have a story. You have a historical story and it needs to be told.

After the story has been told, we see a time of great celebration. It's kind of like our homecoming celebration. There's food and festing. They have come out of their homes into the fields, into temporary shelters to remind them of the blessings of the Lord when they were going across the wilderness area and they lived outdoors. No, they had not been camping out in the wilderness, this was how they lived. God had already promised them a promised land. And what is the need of a promised land without people of promise being in that land? God preserved them, he provided for them and protected them as they traveled from Egypt to where God wanted them to be. The people needed to be reminded, some of them for the first time, of what the Lord had done for them. Then they were filled with thanksgiving.

As we've read in the scriptures, there were several times when God blessed them and they messed up. God blessed them again, they messed up again. And again, and again. Now, we'd be tired of them by now. God gave them a land flowing with milk and honey, and they went and created idols. God blessed them in battle after battle and they turned their nose up at him. If we were in charge, we would have said, Enough. If these were our employees, we'd be writing out pink slips. If these were our relatives, we would have told them what we thought about them and maybe cut them off. But God, in this set of scriptures and throughout the whole Bible, is an entity of love and he kept on giving them another chance. So, where we would be tired of them, we need to be reminding ourselves of how many promises we have made to the Lord Almighty and failed to keep. How many times have we said, Lord, if you save me, I will serve you, but then we didn't do it? A lot of the spirit of the people of God in that time is still in us today. So, we need to be thankful, as they were thankful, for the spirit of forgiveness in Almighty God.

Now that they have been exiled and punished, the elders came up with a plan. The plan was to recommit, to rededicate, do a do-over. That's always appropriate, it's always appropriate to get back in love with God all over again. They came up with some sacred documents and they asked the princes and the leadership to spread these documents abroad, let the people sign them in an organized manner, and present the petition to the Lord. Lord, we re-sign up, we recommit, we rededicate ourselves, we are signing up, as the songwriter has said in modern times, for this Christian jubilee. Are you ready to be re-committed? Yes, we have come short of the glory of God. Do you want to sign up? Do you want to re-enlist in the army of the Lord? Have we gone AWOL? Have we forgotten our first love? Have we gone off after golden calves and things that are shiny and things that sparkle and things that fascinate our attention? Have we considered the world's god as more glitzy and glamorous than our God? Have we decided that the word of God is not as relevant? Have we quit celebrating the word of God that was found in the house of the Lord? Have we stopped taking the time to remember all of his benefits?

Well, today is a good time to re-sign, it is such a good time to re-sign. Think about something you can re-sign up for. Getting to Sunday school on time would be a good thing. Staying for church would be a good thing. Oh, Pastor, that's old-fashioned. It may be, but it's some good stuff, old or new. What are you willing to recommit to the Lord? Your life, your time, your substance? Has your pastor or your teacher been asking you to consider something? Anything from the usher board to the choir, I don't know. What has the Lord been asking you to do? Are you ready? It's time for me and you to re-sign.

Sweet Samples from Scripture

Pastor Walter Henry Cross

Our Response to God's Faithfulness

⁴ The Lord issued the following command to Moses: "Seize all the ringleaders and execute them before the Lord in broad daylight, so his fierce anger will turn away from the people of Israel." ⁵ So Moses ordered Israel's judges, "Each of you must put to death the men under your authority who have joined in worshiping Baal of Peor."

Numbers 25:4-5

In today's lesson, we've got two exciting stories that can bring some light onto our own activity for this day and time. First of all, we see the nation of Israel, you're familiar with them by now, I'm sure. Moses and they are gathered together in the camp. And their camp is out close to the residential area of the Midianites. Well, we know by now that the Israelites were subject to being lured in by foreign and idolatrous gods. This same thing happens again. The Lord has been good to them and they have been bad to God. We need to think about that one. The excitement, the lascivity, and the immorality of the Midianites was attractive to the Israelites and there they went, involving themselves in all that type of activity.

Well the Lord spoke to Moses, the man of God, and said, I am displeased, I am disappointed, I am a jealous God, I want the nation of Israel to be in allegiance to me or I can do a do-over. Now, you don't want the Lord to do a do-over in your life. You want him to start from page one, you don't want him to turn back the pages of time on you and eradicate your existence and start all over. So, the way that Moses interpreted the will of God was that they needed to straighten up and fly right or

they would be no more. This is what happened. The rule went out that all of the leadership, all of the hierarchy, all of those who permitted, tolerated, or stood idly by and did or said nothing while the nation got itself involved in sin and idolatry, would be executed. Preachers, teachers, aren't you glad we don't do that today?

The Lord can and will bring his judgment against all of us who tolerate, look the other way, or become socially and politically correct as in not running anybody off, especially if they're a good financial supporter to the church. But the Bible says preach and stand against sin. And on that day, all of those complicit leaders were executed. The Lord means what he says even to this day. Now, what happened next? One of the leaders of the Israelites came into the camp and he brought a woman of the Moabites with him. His motives were impure. He intended to involve himself and her in an act of immorality. But there was somebody in the camp, a young man of the priestly line, who was also jealous. That means that he was persuaded and passionately embraced the will and the morality of his God to the extent that he sensed the power of God telling him to take action. He interrupted their adulterous and illicit affair with the point of a spear and both of them died with that single blow of the spear. Efficient, but meaningful. When we enjoin ourselves to others who are not in line with the will of God, we bring harm to them and to ourselves. They bring harm to us and we bring harm to them. If we consider ourselves the people of God, we don't need to align ourselves with people who are telling you that they are not.

When we take a look at the second chapter of 1 Samuel, we see what's going on again. The priest at that time, the patriarch of his family, has grown old with years. He's past retirement age and he passes the ministry on to his sons. His sons do wicked in the eyesight of God, in the face of God. Just like the woman and the man who marched through the camp to do evil while others were weeping. They were in your face. They said, God, look at me. I'm going to do this. I don't care what they say, and

I really don't care what you say. I'm going to do this. These two sons of the priest went, as they were preparing the sacrifice at the temple, and they demanded the choicest meat from the sacrifice. They didn't want theirs boiled; it wouldn't taste right. They wanted to roast it. They wanted to have their own prime cuts. They demanded their rights. The people tried to explain to them that the best goes to God. That's still true. The best of whatever you have goes to God. Sacrifice your best to God, to the house of God, to the people of God. Give your best, not something you don't want.

But these men wanted the very best for themselves, and let God take the seconds. How's that for stewardship? This is what happened. They snatched the meat away from the person preparing the altar; they decided that they were bad enough to do whatever they wanted to do. Well, their father had taught them well. They had been warned. And the word of God comes to the father saying, on one day your sadness is going to be double. I'm going to take both your sons the same day. And a series of deaths follows, a lot of violence follows as the Lord God Almighty purges this evil that has invaded the land. God is faithful to his word. He has been faithful to the nation of Israel up until this very moment. And, if we would tell the truth, he has been and still is faithful to us, to me and you. How have we responded?

How did the nation of Israel respond? The Bible says they went off with other idols and other nations. Every time the Lord prepared them for excellence, they did horrific crimes and sinned in the face of God. Now before we talk too bad about them, what are we doing? Check our response. God has blessed us with the beauty of this globe, and we have polluted it in the face of God. God has blessed some of us with a portion of health and strength and we have used that health and strength to do other things than the will of God. We have taken the glory of God and labeled it with our pride. I did this, I said that, that belongs to me, that's mine, that's my property. It all belongs to God. How are we responding this morning

to the blessedness and the faithfulness of Almighty God? We need to think about that.

It's so easy to look at the children of Israel and say, oh, they messed up. It's so easy to look at Hophni and Phinehas, the wicked sons of the priest, and say, oh, they messed up. It's so easy to say, God was right to judge them. He would be right this morning to sit in judgment over us. But mercy and grace, our tag-team attorneys are pleading for us right now. How are you responding to the faithfulness of God? God has kept every promise he's ever made, every last one. He hasn't winked, he hasnt slipped, he hasn't blinked. Everything he's promised us, he has done.

Pastor Walter Henry Cross

Jesus Christ Our Mediator

¹⁴ Work at living in peace with everyone, and work at living a holy life, for those who are not holy will not see the Lord.

Hebrews 12:14

In all of our talking about covenants, sometimes we've talked about the new covenant. The new covenant takes place primarily in the New Testament even though it has its origins in the Old Testament. Remember that Jesus Christ did not do away with the law, but he enhanced and fulfilled the law. So, in chapter 12 of Hebrews, we see mentioned two key words and one of them is peace. In any type of relationship, a covenant relationship, a business relationship, or a personal relationship, peace is very much needed. We need to be peaceable, as far as it lies within us, with everybody. Now let's look at that just a moment: as far as possible, be peaceable. That's where the power of the Holy Spirit comes in to help us live in peace with our brothers and sisters, boys and girls, people throughout our family, our home, our community, and the world. If we look at the newspaper and at the news media, we find out that there's a lot of peace breakers in the world, a lot of broken peace around. We are not adhering to the Word of God where he asked us to be peaceable as far as it lies within us. As far as I have to do anything with it, let me be the one who is bringing forth peace as a Christian believer.

The second word in this chapter that's very interesting is holiness. We are to live holy in the sight of our Lord. We are to be people of holiness. That doesn't mean we ought to be

unusual but it does mean that we should be different from the norm if the norm means worldliness. So, we are to be holy, our lives should be holy. That word scares some of us because we think of it as a denomination, but it's actually a lifestyle, it's a lifestyle of adhering to the Word of God. It's not scary, it's not frightening, it's not necessarily emotional, it's not necessarily emotionless, it is a lifestyle of adhering to the Word of God. The power of the Holy Spirit comes alongside and enables us to live in such a way that our Heavenly Father, our God Almighty, views us through the blood of Jesus in what I refer to as positional holiness.

So, we are to be holy, our lives should be holy.

Those are two elements, peace and holiness, that are very necessary in this new covenant that is a spiritual covenant. We've talked about promises of land, promises of heritage, promises of legacy, and promises of nationhood. Now we're talking about a promise of spiritual growth and maturity in the body of Christ. We're talking about eternal life. We're going into a new country, not Jerusalem here on earth, but the New Jerusalem is coming down to us. We're going to a far better country. The book of Hebrews deals with the supremacy of Christ and this is brought out as he is titled, in this lesson, the mediator, the one, the man in the middle, the go-between.

In the next few verses in this chapter, we revisit that fiery mountain, that occasion where the people were frightened, where they were upset because of the billowing smoke and the fire and the sound of the trumpets. Moses is quoted as saying, I'm scared myself, I'm going to go up here and meet God and I'm a little shaky about this. This was where the commandments came and even the animals were forbidden to touch this holy mountain this holy space. If they accidentally got in there, they had to be executed, they had to be slaughtered because nothing profane or common could touch this place of God.

Now, that presents a divine problem, or opportunity is the way I like to look at it. How can man make contact with God, which is needful for our existence, if God is untouchable, if God is a mountain of fire, if God is billowing in such a holy place that our common-ness cannot coexist with the holiness of God? That's where Jesus comes in as a mediator. He holds our hand and holds God's hand. That's the way we used to say it when we were in school and that makes it real simple. He grabs a hold of us and grabs a hold of God and makes that holy connection between mankind, humankind, and the divinity of God. He's our mediator. He goes before us, he's our Shepherd, he leads us, he leads us into all areas of truth.

> **If we are believers baptized into the holiness of Christ, we are in relationship with God the Father. And to be in relationship with Almighty God, we must also be in fellowship with humankind.**

So, now the mountain is no longer untouchable because we are in Jesus Christ. This is a beautiful lesson. If we are believers baptized into the holiness of Christ, we are in relationship with God the Father. And to be in relationship with Almighty God, we must also be in fellowship with humankind. Look again at this entire chapter, it is rich.

I want you to think about how you have made a new connection with people who may be difficult to live peaceably with. Then we have a greater understanding of how God has, through his Son, Jesus Christ, through the blood of Jesus, made it possible for us because he is that sacrifice. Back out on the plains of Sinai, they used animals for sacrifice, but they were temporary sacrifices. Now, there's a permanent sacrifice and it is in the

person of Jesus Christ, so through his blood we make that connection. But to help understand how important connection is, think about a time when you have dealt with someone who was not peaceable but then you revisited the situation and made peace with them. Remember, Pastor always says that you're not responsible how they respond to you, but you are responsible for how you respond to them. That's a testimony that will last forever. Jesus Christ, our mediator. He is the man in the middle, he's our go-between, he makes the connection.

A Promise to Remember

¹¹ But among the Lord's people, women are not independent of men, and men are not independent of women. ¹² For although the first woman came from man, every other man was born from a woman, and everything comes from God.

1 Corinthians 11:11-12

We have agreed over the last several lessons that a covenant is a promise. A divine covenant is a promise from God and a promise from God is unique from any other type of agreement between humankind because God has chosen not to go back on his word, God has chosen not to ever do anything that's contrary to what he's already said. If God said it, he will do it. He speaks truth and he does not stutter. It's very important to note that when God makes you a promise, it's a promise that you can be assured of.

In this lesson, we're talking about holy communion, the Lord's table, Holy Eucharist, the great Thanksgiving. All of these words have to do with that time in church that you might be familiar with. It's a time that we pass around a small portion of bread, or we go forward and receive a little crust of bread, depending on your religious community. You may pull the bread from the loaf signifying unity, or you may be passed out a little piece of that crusty bread, a little thin wafer that indicates the body of our Lord and Savior Jesus Christ. There's also the cup, the cup that we lift up that symbolizes the shed blood of Jesus on Calvary.

Chapter 11 of 1 Corinthians starts off with divine order. God has an order to nearly everything that we do in life religiously, or inside the family, or how we order our steps day to day. In this chapter there's some troubling areas for some people who have preconceived notions that they bring to the Bible, not take away from the Bible. One of the things that we see is the order of the relationship between God and between Jesus and between husband and between wife or woman. Now if God is using, and I believe that he is, the structure of heaven as a prototype for the family here on earth, the woman is not subservient to the man. Follow me now. Jesus Christ is the son of Almighty God, yet Jesus Christ said he was equal to God. The Bible in this fashion says that the man is the head of the woman but does not say that the woman is subservient. She is a wonderfully, divinely made, individual creation of Almighty God, yet there's order.

There's order in the heavenlies and there's order on earth for things to be accomplished. It doesn't mean less than. You can be equal to but still have order, like in the military. Some of the smartest people on the field are people who graduated from military academies but they give their allegiance to the men and women who may be career staff sergeants on the field because the sergeants know what to do next. Wisdom is knowing what to do next. They have the experience, they have more to them than just a degree for military science. They have on-the-ground experience. A wise lieutenant or colonel will give their attention to the person who has experience because this saves lives. Order saves life. So, don't get hung up on thinking that God is trying to rank the relationship in the human sphere. What God is doing through Paul is setting up order. Order is good.

What we really want to focus on now is the covenant of the Lord's table. Jesus said do this, as oft as you do it, which in indication of frequency, how often you do it. Do it regularly, do it often, do it regularly, once a month, twice a month, every Sunday, every day, I wouldn't have any problem with that, but as oft as you do it, when you do it, do it regularly, remember me. Remember that sacrifice. That's how important the first Sunday of the month is. For some churches it may be the fourth Sunday or whatever Sunday you choose to celebrate this memorial meal, that little crust of bread and a little portion of a cup of the fruit of the vine. What's the meaning behind this meager meal? The meaning is that I remember that the only unique, the only begotten Son of God laid down his life. He surrendered his body to brutality and shed his blood because of violence, because of my sin. Jesus simply says I want you to remember that, how much I love you, how much the Father loves you.

Now, listen. Paul had to correct some things for the Corinthians. One of the things that was going on was that there were classes. The people came together and those who had did not share with the ones who had not. The ones who had would sit at their table, like they used to do in the high school cafeteria and laugh and poke fun at the ones who didn't have the same type of food or didn't have any food. At the table I sat at in the school, everybody had something to eat. Whether they brought it with them or not, before they left the table everybody had something to eat. That's fellowship, that's *koinonia*, that's the love that Jesus wants celebrated at his table. Let whosoever will come to this table, there are no restrictions. Come and drink, come and eat and be full. Allow the practice of communion at the Lord's table to fill you every time you experience it and leave wherever you are differently than the way you came in.

One other thing about communion. There's a warning in this chapter associated with it. The warning is, come to the table right. Be in good relationship with your friends and relatives. This is a time for fellowship. All of us have an opinion and some of you have some wonderful opinions that are better than mine, but when we come together, we come together for fellowship and unity. When you come to the table, it's not for a party, or to get drunk. That's what Paul is telling the people

because that was their practice. You're not coming together to be showy. Paul was telling the people that because that was their practice, too. You're not coming together to eat up all the food before the other people get there. So, Paul is talking to them and to us. This table of Holy Communion, this table of remembrance, this table of honor and worship, changes me and if you let it, it'll change you. What are you doing to bring about fellowship? What are you doing to bring about unity? Remember, communion is not associated with a curse. I know some who stay away from church on communion because they would tell me, well, I just wasn't living right. That's the time to go. You don't go to the hospital when you feel good. You don't go to the emergency room when you feel like running and jumping and flipping over. You go when you have a medical need. So, when we have a spiritual need, we go to church. Before we have communion, in my experience, there's always an opportunity for prayer for repentance for cleansing. So, go. Pray the prayer of repentance. Be cleansed by the power of the Holy Spirit and receive the body of Christ. Think about that today. Think about the barriers to communion. Let's do our best to bring about Holy Communion and remember the sacrifice of Christ. We can also remember it by sacrificing what we have to share with others.

Pastor Walter Henry Cross

Faith and Joy

Sweet Samples from Scripture

Pastor Walter Henry Cross

Faith That Brings Joy

⁷ Then Peter took the lame man by the right hand and helped him up. And as he did, the man's feet and ankles were instantly healed and strengthened. ⁸ He jumped up, stood on his feet, and began to walk! Then, walking, leaping, and praising God, he went into the Temple with them. ⁹ All the people saw him walking and heard him praising God. ¹⁰ When they realized he was the lame beggar they had seen so often at the Beautiful Gate, they were absolutely astounded! ¹¹ They all rushed out in amazement to Solomon's Colonnade, where the man was holding tightly to Peter and John. ¹² Peter saw his opportunity and addressed the crowd. "People of Israel," he said, "what is so surprising about this? And why stare at us as though we had made this man walk by our own power or godliness?

Acts 3:7-12

I want to talk with you about faith and faithfulness. One of the things that I want to share with you is that faith is the very act of trusting God. It's the action that's associated with a belief system that allows me and you to trust, rest, and rely upon the name of Jesus Christ. Faith. In Acts, the third chapter, down around verse 11, we find the Apostles, the special messengers, Peter and John as they make their way to worship. They have encountered a man that was lame or disabled or otherwise abled from birth. His lower extremities did not allow him the ability to be independently mobile. Possibly his muscles, by this time as a young adult or as an adult male, had atrophied, his bones probably were brittle, the joints maybe were stiff, frozen by time and some type of position, maybe

the lowest position or some other position that was frozen in place, and his mobility probably was dependent upon others who could not afford to take care of him. He could not afford to take care of himself so he was often taken to a public place, the entrance of the temple where there was a lot of traffic, especially around holidays, and where others who were passing by could look upon him and look upon his inability to make it for himself and contribute to his cause. These men of God came by, spoke words of faith and healing to him, and he became whole. The Bible says he leaped up. There was no physical therapy. There was no time for him to recover. He became whole instantly. Because of that he held on in a loving embrace of gratitude to the Apostles.

The people, the Israelites, as referred to in some translations, observed this miracle and they were amazed as you and I would be at the miraculous healing. Instantly the blood flow was restored to his lower extremities. Instantly the knees became pliable and like butter, and the joints moved with ease. Not only did he have the ability to stand, and it doesn't say he was wobbly, he might have been, but the Bible doesn't say that, but he could leap for joy. He could celebrate. He could worship and he could indicate his extreme gratitude for what the Lord had done to him through the men of God.

Let's touch this just for a moment. Celebration worship does not have to be emotional or filled with physical frenzy, but if the Lord would restore my vision or my impediments or my ability to walk and stand unassisted or whatever your impediment or mine may be, if that happened to me instantly, you might read somewhere that old Pastor Cross was jumping for joy, leaping for joy. That's just me, that's not something you have to do. That's just me, that'd be the way I would respond to the miracle of healing.

Now the faith comes in concerning the people. The men of God challenged them. Why are you so amazed? Do you trust the God of your fathers? Do you trust the God you've been taught

about in rabbinical school? Do you believe that this miracle was not the power of God? Do you believe that God was not able? Then why are you surprised? Why are you shocked? Why are you so amazed at God doing what God already does? So, let's ask ourselves this: Do we ever become amazed that God does it again? That he touches us again? That he touches our loved ones again? Surely, it's a time for celebration and acknowledgement, but our faith level should be growing and maturing to the point that we expect, anticipate the miracle working of God in our lives personally and in the lives of others. Our faith should be growing. Our ability to believe that God would do what God has said he would do should be growing until we have a sense of expectant hope.

We should hope for a change. You think everything is going to continue to be the way it is? No sir, no ma'am, God is going to bring an end to this, God is going to bring a change to this. What's going on in your life will not always be like it's going on today, have faith. Something is going to happen, and if God has anything to do with it, it's going to be something great. They challenged the Israelites, the men of God challenged them and reminded them of their sin, the sin of rejection, the historic sin that they'd rather have Barabbas than Jesus. They made a choice, a politically motivated choice that they'd rather have someone who had possessed and confessed of being evil in order to eliminate this Jesus who was putting a crimp in their style.

My brothers and sisters, faith in Almighty God will give us the ability to accept what Jesus is doing. Maybe we don't see it, maybe don't agree with it, maybe we're having trouble acknowledging it, but we need to know beyond a shadow of a doubt that if Jesus is Jesus, he's Jesus enough for whatever is wrong in our lives. He has risen from the sleep of death. The Bible says, and this is very encouraging in this group of verses, that he's getting ready to come back when everything is put in place. God is still working on us. Have faith. He's still making

changes in your life, in my life. Have faith. He's still doing the miraculous, he's still healing. Have faith. Well preacher, it's not happening to me, it's not happening in a timely manner. Have faith in God. Everything is not restored yet. But have faith that it's going to be done.

I want you to think about the bridge that faith has taken you across in life. Those things where you didn't see a way. You didn't see an answer. You were in a predicament that you could not get yourself out of. But the miraculous happened. Tell it over again and it's going to encourage you. Faith will bring joy to your life. Sometimes our circumstances and situations and uncontrollable conditions don't change immediately, but our attitude can change by having a reliance and belief in the power of Almighty God through His Son Jesus Christ empowered by the person of the Holy Spirit. Have faith and joy today.

Pastor Walter Henry Cross

Faith That Unlocks Understanding

² One day as these men were worshiping the Lord and fasting, the Holy Spirit said, "Appoint Barnabas and Saul for the special work to which I have called them." ³ So after more fasting and prayer, the men laid their hands on them and sent them on their way.

Acts 13:2-3

In chapter 13 of Acts, we see a special occasion taking place. There is a celebration, what we would call an ordination, where the power of God through the person of the Holy Spirit speaks to the church. They were gathered there after being involved in three very significant things. Worship, prayer, and fasting. They were seeking to make a decision on leadership in terms of missionary journeys and going out and telling other people about Christ. It was very sacred, it was very special. Ordination means simply the recognition by the church and the celebration of the church of what God has already done in the lives of others. They laid hands on them as a sign of commissioning and approval and authority. So the power of God being active in this young church, after the present leadership made the decision to go into a season of worship and prayer and fasting, the Holy Spirit indicated to them that they needed to set aside Paul and Barnabas to go forth and to make disciples. In this part of our text, sometimes Paul is referred to as Saul.

Let's talk a little bit about fasting. Sometimes the best way to define something is to tell you what it's not. It is not a diet program. It is not a weight-loss program. It is when

we determine in our spirit, being led by the spirit, that we need a time of intimacy with the Lord. And that intimacy is so important that we don't spend a lot of time eating or watching television or dealing with our devices or dealing with distractions. It's a special time that we set aside to have intimacy with the Lord. We don't go out and brag about it. We don't tell people how many days and how many hours and how many doughnuts we passed up. Fasting creates intimacy. It's when we decide that we are going to keep the refrigerator closed and the stove cold and the microwave closed for a season. Now if you're diabetic, and if you have certain medical situations, you need to consult your doctor. You need to be wise, we don't need to be foolish, you need to explore with your pastor or some of your religious leaders concerning what is a denial, what is a fast, and what's good for you. This lesson is about discernment and discernment is holy understanding. This is another area where we need holy understanding. Making yourself sick is not of God, but setting aside certain distractions in life, sometimes there are some necessary distractions, but when you make that decision to set aside certain distractions in life so you can spend more time with the Lord, your life is going to be empowered again by the presence of the Holy Spirit.

Well Paul and Barnabas went out on the journey. They went into various parts that they have been assigned to travel in and to win souls for Christ. And on one occasion they ran into a person by the name of Bar-Jesus. Jesus was a common name and Bar means son of. He probably was not related to our Jesus Christ, but it was a very common name like John or George or any name like that. But this particular person was involved in sorcery, involved in the occult, involved in something similar to witchcraft. Now sorcery is the base word where we get pharmaceutical from so he would be equivalent to a drug dealer, or a root doctor in my neck of the woods. He was a person who was a false teacher. He was telling people that he had powers that he did not have. He had some power invested in him by the power of darkness. He was a trickster,

he was a confidence man, he could do illusions. He decided he needed to get close to the government official in that province. He understood something that we need to understand and that is that influence is better than power. He didn't have the position of governor, but he wanted to share in the power of the governor, so he was always close around. He was close around the governor's palace and when it came time for lunch or a banquet, his seat was close.

Then comes along these two preachers, Barnabas and Saul, full of the Holy Spirit. The governor became curious and sent for them. I want you to come and tell me about God. Since he was fake and phony, this sorcerer, this Bar-Jesus, decided that he was going to influence the governor. Don't let those folks come up in here, they're going to tell you a whole lot of stuff, they're going to mess up your mind, they're going to preach to you, and you're going to go insane and crazy. You don't need that, you're a good governor, you don't need any of that kind of stuff.

The Bible says the men of God looked at him. Oh, I hope you can sense what's going on right now. Let me tell you a story. I was in church one time and I was probably three or four years old. I've always been fascinated with church bulletins because they were made out of this stiff paper. And I thought, sitting there next to my mother, that this church bulletin would make the best paper airplane in the world. It was stiff, I began to fold it, I made those creases, it was sharp on the point, it had the wing spread I wanted. I even poked a little hole out where you can put your finger and launch it. Then my mother looked at me. She turned, she didn't say a word, she looked at me. Now at three or four years old I don't claim that I was all that spiritual, but I discerned her look. I understood her look and I began to press that bulletin back out; I took those creases back out and I sat there. I had a degree of divine understanding what my mother meant when she looked at me. Well, this fake and phony fella received that look and some words. Why are you twisting the truth? Why are you trying to lead good people astray? The

Bible says that the governor was an intelligent man. That's a good quality, if you're going to be in government, to be a critical thinker. This was an intelligent man. Suddenly, through the power of God, words were spoken to this fake fellow. You're going to become blind, you're going to lose your sight. You've been leading people astray, now people are going to lead you for a while so you can understand the vulnerability of being led around by somebody who you think is taking you in the right direction. The governor saw it, the governor was amazed, and the governor became a believer.

Let's talk about unleasing the Holy Spirit today. What's the key in this lesson? Prayer, worship, and fasting. Then you will get the gift of discernment. Now, some people have it to a greater degree than others and they go around and say, I have the gift of discernment. But it's not something that needs to be foreign to any of us. If we use that precious key of being in relationship with the Lord on an intimate level, the Lord will reward us with the power of holy understanding, and we won't be led astray. Think about some times when you couldn't figure it out, you couldn't work it out, but through what you would consider, after this lesson, divine understanding, or discernment, you had faith in the decision that God had impressed you with. Tell the young people, tell other people how God will help you figure out what is baffling and confusing in your life today.

The Faith to Continue

19 Then some Jews arrived from Antioch and Iconium and won the crowds to their side. They stoned Paul and dragged him out of town, thinking he was dead. 20 But as the believers gathered around him, he got up and went back into the town.

Acts 14:19-20

The book of Acts is like a manual as to how we should do church. It tells about the foundation and growth of the new church. We can glean from that book in the New Testament how we can be about doing evangelism, doing church start, and maintaining the gospel within our church and without. Very helpful. It gives us a lot of insight into leadership development and how to be good stewards of the resources that the Lord has given us. Acts chapter 14 opens up with something that we have been aware of before. That's the miracle of healing. Note, bear in mind, understand that the miraculous healings that God gave during that time of the beginning of the church had the purpose of drawing men and women and boys and girls to their need of the gospel, to their need of a savior, to their need of Jesus Christ. Today, when the Lord does something miraculous in our lives, we need to testify of the goodness of the Lord. We need to tell somebody. Don't stand up in church and be disruptive if that's not your church tradition but pray and ask the Lord through the power of the Holy Spirit and you will be given an opportunity. Maybe on the bus stop, maybe in the cafeteria, it may be in some unknown place while you're getting your oil changed, the Lord will give you that

opportunity to share the miraculous in your life because it draws people toward him.

Now this has taken place, another miracle of healing, a man lame from birth. He gets up, leaps up. He's running and jumping and excited about having power in his legs he never had before. Well, don't you know, everybody was not happy about that. In fact, some other people came to town and persuaded and influenced the crowd that saw this miracle to think negatively about Paul and his companion, his ministerial companion, Barnabas. They seized Paul. They attacked him and beat him and stoned him within an inch of his life. Thinking he was dead, they dragged him outside of the city for the buzzards to come and devour his body. The disciples, and this is what disciples should do even today, gathered around their fallen comrade. I would assume they prayed to the Lord. Miraculously, Paul gets up and he continues his ministerial journey. He goes to other areas in that region and he preaches the gospel. He preaches of salvation even with the scars on his face and on his body, bearing the wounds of being a pioneer for Jesus Christ. He was out there, and he suffered because of it but he kept on preaching. Faith to continue, faith to persevere.

He preaches of salvation even with the scars on his face and on his body, bearing the wounds of being a pioneer for Jesus Christ.

As time went by, our brother said something that stirs in my spirit. He said, Let us return. Now, if I was one of the disciples, I would say, Return where? Let's go back to this certain place. Now let me understand, you want to go back to the place where you were seized, where you were attacked, where you were beaten within an inch of your life, where you were thrown outside of the city thinking you were dead? You want to go back there? Yes. And he did. He went back to encourage the men and women that you're going to go up against opposition, you're going to have trouble, and sometimes, Sunday school scholars, you have to return to the fight. You have to return. I don't mean for you to be contentious. I don't want you to get involved in fisticuffs in the middle of a worship service. I don't want you to disrupt the administrative council or some business meeting at the church just to get your point across. But if you are contending for the faith, if you are on a mission for the Lord to tell the truth about Jesus Christ, sometimes you have to return to places where you've been rejected. You have to return, in a loving way, maybe to a family member, maybe to a church member, maybe to a non-church person that you work with or that you met at the barbershop. You have to allow the spirit to give you a method of what to say and how to say it to address this issue again without creating hostility.

He left again, but what is so exciting to me is that he had the faith to continue.

He returned to the scene of the crime. He kept on preaching. Now, he was wise, he didn't linger long. He left again, but what is so exciting to me is that he had the faith to continue. So many of us have given up. We have taken on YouTube and we've taken on the television and there's wonderful, wonderful word teaching in these various mediums of digital and video outlets. They're wonderful. They're wonderful. But now, if you're staying at home because you were pressing for what the Lord told you to do and it was not received, and you grabbed your marbles and ran to the house, you need to go back. If you're upset because somebody didn't see it your way and you know your way was right, you need to go back. If you are sitting and sulking and souring because somebody is not agreeing with you and maybe they're even throwing stones of lies and slander towards you, go back. Go back until God dismisses you from that place.

You'll know when you've been dismissed. Haven't we talked about the faith to understand what God wants you to know? God will give you another assignment but more than likely the assignment won't be for you to go home. Stay in the fight. Return to the scene of the crime. Have the faith to keep on keeping on. Have the faith to persevere. Have there been assignments that God has given you and you have abandoned? It may be time to go back.

Pastor Walter Henry Cross

Faith That Makes a Difference

¹ Therefore I, a prisoner for serving the Lord, beg you to lead a life worthy of your calling, for you have been called by God. ² Always be humble and gentle. Be patient with each other, making allowance for each other's faults because of your love. ³ Make every effort to keep yourselves united in the Spirit, binding yourselves together with peace. ⁴ For there is one body and one Spirit, just as you have been called to one glorious hope for the future. ⁵ There is one Lord, one faith, one baptism, ⁶ one God and Father of all, who is over all, in all, and living through all.

Epsesians 4:1-6

Paul is writing to the church at Ephesus. Paul is incarcerated in jail for doing good. Have you ever been punished for doing good? Then you understand what's going on with Paul. Paul is writing to the church. Now we have the communication in part. We have the answers to the questions, we have the instruction that's given for what Paul has received by carrier, by messenger, by friend, by word-of-mouth, by someone who has come to him, visited him while he was incarcerated, and said, let me tell you what's going on at the church. And it was not all good. There was a sense of division. People had aligned themselves according to certain personalities. They had begun to involve themselves in the practice of legalism that was a part of their life before they heard about the truth that is the gospel and the freedom that's in the gospel.

So, Paul was helping them to correct themselves. He first starts out by saying, when we were together, we talked the talk and now it's your opportunity as the church of God to walk the walk. Walk worthy. And that comes home to us today. We are to walk worthy of the calling that God has called us, the assignment. We need to walk like we know Jesus. Now, we do pretty good about talking about it, we put up a good talk. But Paul said, Live like it. That's what that word walk means. Your conversation, your lifestyle, your habits, your association, the people you hang out with. All of that needs to resemble the fact that you are acquainted with Jesus Christ. We need to know beyond a shadow of a doubt that we are exemplifying and projecting the power of Christ out of our lives into others.

Paul said simply, you're living beneath your privilege. There's so many of us that do that today. We act like we don't know we're blessed. We act like we don't know that the Word has broken every chain. We act like we don't know that we are dealing with a resurrected Savior who's not in a tomb. Walk worthy, he said. And then he told them, do away with the stuff that's dividing you. Be intentional, deal with the relationship and not with the issues, embrace each other. We must do away with the stuff that divides. You know man came up with all these denominations, we don't see that in the Bible anywhere. I don't fight denominations as long as people are preaching and receiving the truth and the freedom of the gospel concerning Jesus Christ. But there's division that's wrong. We divide ourselves over how we baptize, we divide ourselves over the color of the carpet, we divide ourselves over what the choir is going to sing on Sunday, or over which boy is going to usher. Or we'll come to church if so-and-so is preaching or if so-and-so is not preaching. Paul said, You're wrong about that. That does not give an illustration to the world as to who Jesus is. He told us that the methodology for us to utilize in terms of conquering all these divisions is be love. We need to love each other in the most holy faith. A second criteria that he put out is that we should also not only love each other in the true holiness that's complete and without any type of sidestepping, but we also need to be aware and obey the will of God. We need to be in his word, we need to be in his will, and we need to be in his way.

We do not need to be beneath our privilege. We are blessed, we need to know it, and we need to live like it. We need to love each other. We can have differences. We can have different ideas, different persuasions, different notions, but we ought not to break up and fall out about it to the extent that we tell the world we can't get along. We can't invite the world into our mess. So, we need to be unified. That takes faith. What did I say faith was, you remember? Faith is the very act of trusting God. We need to become vulnerable. It is risk-taking to have faith in relationships, to make yourself vulnerable, to make yourself get out there on the limb and love someone and not require them to do anything in exchange for that love back. That's what Paul is saying we need to do. We need to trust God with these issues and ideas and these various things that we come up with. We need to trust God and love God and know that the Lord we serve can and will make a difference.

How can you make a difference? I want you to become aware of the fact that the Lord that we serve can do more with me and you at this present time than has happened all of our lives up until now if we yield ourselves to him, if we love each other, and if we become mature and grow up. That takes grace, that takes love, that takes intentionality, that takes a willing heart. You can change this world one person at a time, but first we have to deal with ourselves.

Sweet Samples from Scripture

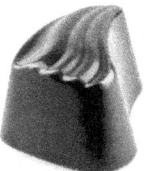

Pastor Walter Henry Cross

The Faith to Have Convictions

⁸ But Daniel was determined not to defile himself by eating the food and wine given to them by the king. He asked the chief of staff for permission not to eat these unacceptable foods.

Daniel 1:8

As we talk about faith, we're going back into the Old Testament, or the first dispensation, and have Daniel as our guide. Daniel is a young man in the Old Testament that we talk a lot about and preach a lot of sermons about. You remember him in the lions' den and things of that nature. One of the things we're going to talk about with Daniel is the faith to have convictions. Now, my brothers and sisters, young men and young ladies, and boys and girls, a lot of us have opinions. But if we truly understand the Word of God, we formulate convictions. Opinions can change. Opinions are waiting for a challenge. Opinions are waiting for some new idea. But Jesus loves me, this I know. I don't have an opinion about it, I know. I don't have just an idea about it, I know from my experience with him. I know that Jesus loves me, and I'm convinced and convicted of that. That's my conviction. I have the trust in God to believe beyond the shadow of a doubt that my conviction is built on a solid rock.

Let's look at what's going on with Daniel in the first twelve verses of Daniel chapter one. Egypt had made war against Babylon. The Egyptians failed in their attempt but because Jerusalem and the Jews supported the Egyptians, Nebuchadnezzar decided to siege and invade Jerusalem as

punishment for their previous alliance. It was political, it was strategic and during this time of the siege of Jerusalem, his father passed away. He had to rush back over 500 miles to get to his kingdom in order to secure his position as heir to the throne. But before he left, he gave some very solid instructions. I want my assistants, my deputies, my princes, to go into Jerusalem. I want you to collect the strongest men, the smartest men, and the best-looking young men and bring them to Babylon. What was he going to do with them when they got there? Well, he wanted them to be trained for a three-year period, to involve themselves in physical strengthening, to learn a new language, to be aware of the government and the culture, and even the food, so that he could raise them up as followers of an idol god. Sometimes this worship was of himself, which still would be an idol. He wanted them to take their places in his entourage of men of note, men of valor and intelligence.

So, Daniel, accompanied by four that we know of, probably many more, but we know the names of four of them, was positioned to be groomed by the king and the king's men. They even had certain dietary restrictions. The king wanted them to eat the king's own food so that they would get fat and strong and powerful for use in this idolatrous country. What did Daniel say? He had the faith to stand strong by his convictions. There is a lesson there for us. Do we have opinions, or do we have convictions? They wanted him to eat the meat, the food, and the wine from the king's table. He said no. Food that's probably more expensive than he could afford back home. He said no. Food that probably was cooked to perfection and seasoned well and garnished well and that had an excellent aroma. But he said no, ask the king if he will allow us to eat vegetables. Now, my brothers and sisters, there's a plug right there for a plant-based diet. I'm not going to kick against that. That's something that I am interested in as well. I haven't given up chicken wings yet but y'all pray with me about that. I see value in a plant-based diet. But the idea here is, do you trust God? Daniel said, yes, I trust God and I'm going to turn away from the king's

table. Allow me to eat just vegetables, then come back and test me. Come and see, come and let me weigh in, come and let me participate in calisthenics. Let me show you what God can do if I remain faithful to God Jehovah.

Well, he was allowed the privilege of rejecting the king's food and the end result was that he was stronger, he was healthier, he was even mentally more alert than the other young men that got their diet, their nutrition from the king's table. It didn't seem that he was lacking in anything and the other young man with him were the same. This is our lesson for today, trust God. Develop convictions. Something that is true to your core, that you won't waver about the next time someone calls you on the phone and gives you another idea. You won't become doubtful the next time a situation or circumstances and conditions get out of your control. You won't turn around at the first spiritual exit that you come to.

Convictions take faith, active trust in God. Convictions are not opinions. They are your core beliefs, and nobody can make you believe otherwise. That's the way I feel about Jesus the Christ. There are a lot of skeptics who write about Daniel and they say that this book of prophecy that talks about end times is so accurate that the only way it could have been written is after the fact. Well, I don't believe that. I believe the Bible is the Bible. I believe the Bible is the Word of God and I believe it's true, as my grandmother would say, from cover to cover. I still believe that, and I believe that Daniel was inspired by the power of God through the spirit to write down a very detailed and accurate report of what was happening which has been proven through archaeology. As late as 1956, they actually found the banquet hall where they had this big party that we talk about so much in Daniel. They found the actual, place no one could make that up. So, Daniel is very accurate, very prophetic.

What is Daniel telling me, what is he telling you? Have convictions in the face of something that's threatening, like the king's armed men ordering you to eat this food, to say no, I

won't do it, I love the Lord and I trust him. The end result will be victory. I want you to think about the times when you have moved from opinion, what I think, to conviction, what I know. I believe too many of us are hanging on to maybe I think, maybe I should, maybe I should have. But when you ever get to the point of having certainty in Christ, not in yourself, but having certainty in Christ, you'll be getting to the point of having core convictions. Can't nobody at that point turn you around.

Pastor Walter Henry Cross

Fireproof Faith

16 Shadrach, Meshach, and Abednego replied, "O Nebuchadnezzar, we do not need to defend ourselves before you. 17 If we are thrown into the blazing furnace, the God whom we serve is able to save us. He will rescue us from your power, Your Majesty. 18 But even if he doesn't, we want to make it clear to you, Your Majesty, that we will never serve your gods or worship the gold statue you have set up."

28 Then Nebuchadnezzar said, "Praise to the God of Shadrach, Meshach, and Abednego! He sent his angel to rescue his servants who trusted in him. They defied the king's command and were willing to die rather than serve or worship any god except their own God. 29 Therefore, I make this decree: If any people, whatever their race or nation or language, speak a word against the God of Shadrach, Meshach, and Abednego, they will be torn limb from limb, and their houses will be turned into heaps of rubble. There is no other god who can rescue like this!" 30 Then the king promoted Shadrach, Meshach, and Abednego to even higher positions in the province of Babylon.

Daniel 3:16-18, 28-30

In the third chapter of Daniel, we have another lesson about faith. Nebuchadnezzar was the king. He was the person in that particular area who was large and in charge. He had been successful in battle and had made a decision to go through Jerusalem, a defeated area, and cherry-pick the best and the brightest individuals from that region to take them into captivity and train them to be part of his entourage in his own personal world, his own personal kingdom. We've talked about a challenge that Daniel and some of his Hebrew friends had

because the king wanted them to eat certain things and drink certain things in order that they would become strong and vital and useful in his kingdom. Daniel and the Hebrew followers of God Yahweh made a decision that they would stand with God, the God that they served, the only true and living God, and not abide by the King's wishes. They went counter-cultural, even in captivity. That took some extraordinary faith, and we talked about that faith to just make a stand.

Now, there are times when we are called upon to go counter-cultural today. It's not going to be popular. It may be threatening. You may have people standing around you with a different opinion and their opinion may be as sharp as a two-edged sword. But we have discovered that convictions are better than opinions. So, now we're going to talk about fireproof faith. Faith is the very act of trusting God and it's going to be tested. It has been tested in your life and it will be tested in your life. It's being tested right now. Do we have a fireproof faith?

Here's the scenario, here's the story. The king is getting a little bit bored, so he decides to do something. After defeating all of these countries he wants everybody to bow down to this image, a statute that he has built that glitters in the sun. Maybe his ego needed some pumping up, so he ordered this statue to be built. He ordered a band to play and when the sound of the noise and the music went forth, all of the conquered nations and his subjects were to bow down. He had all of the hierarchy of his government and the governors and the senators and the Congress people, that would be our equivalent, and everyone all the way down to the royal dog-catcher, they were all there. When the sound went forth, they were to fall prostrate and laid out in front of this statue just because the king wanted it done. He wanted personal worship.

Now, there were some individuals who were sneaking around looking. There's some in every organization, every family, every system. They're just looking to see what they can see with no good motive in mind. So, they were looking around and they saw that the Hebrew gentlemen did not bow down to this

idolatrous image. They didn't bend their knee, they didn't bow their head. They knew that the God they served was sufficient. Well they snuck around and got an audience with the king and they said, O king, wonderful king, live forever. A lot of times when people are bringing you dirt, they start off with a compliment. You're such a good man, you're a good deacon, you're not like the rest of those brothers, you're not like the rest of those sisters, you're the best pastor we ever had. They told the other pastors the same thing, I guarantee.

So, that's what they said. O wonderful King, I happened to notice just the other day when I was passing by, I saw your Hebrew gentlemen were not bowing down at the sound of the trumpet. They were not following your orders, they were not giving allegiance to this golden beautiful statue that you put up. And the king said, say what? They're not doing what? Well the king now feels embarrassed. He brought these individuals into the kingdom, he has given them positions of authority and now he finds out through the backdoor that they are not bowing down to his image. All of a sudden, his pride flashes in front of him and he said, they're going to do what I tell them to do. Now, there are pastors who believe that. I made you a deacon, now you're going to do what I tell you to do. I made you a secretary, you're going to do what I tell you to do. I made you an usher, you're going to do what I tell you to do. That's God's prerogative, that's God's prerogative. You're not God, pastors, teachers, remember you're not God in anybody's life. You are a road sign pointing them to Almighty God.

Well, the king got full of himself, he got drunk on the wine of pride. All of a sudden, he found himself ordering them to bow before the statue or face a fiery death. You need fireproof faith when you're facing the fiery challenge. These Hebrew gentlemen gave us something that has given us courage all of our lives. They said, if our God, the only true and living God, decides to save us, we're going to come out of the fire praising him. If he decides to embrace us unto himself, we're going on to be with

him. Win-win situation. If you want to put the devil on the run in your life, move to win-win. If the Lord decides to say yes, thank you Jesus. If the Lord decides to say no, thank you Jesus. If you praise him for whatever, Satan can't do anything with that. That's why we need fireproof faith.

Well, this egomaniac became angry. He ordered that the fiery furnace be heated seven times hotter. I don't know what the temperature was but it was the case of being so hot that some of the individuals tending the fire, that were assigned to execute these men of God, became asphyxiated by the fire and died trying to throw these young men in. These three Hebrews went in. The King looked and he looked and in the fire he saw four. Then something happened to him on the inside. He said I thought I ordered you all to put three in, now why is there four? And this fourth one looked different. When people see you accepting and dealing with your challenge with fireproof faith, they notice the godly difference. They don't notice me and you, but they notice the godliness that's in and around us. So, the king goes to the opening of the furnace and he said send them out and he calls them. They come out and he said the God, and this is important, the God that you all serve allowed you to offer up your body without any certainty and serve him in the midst of calamity. I want all of my nations, all of my servants, not to say or utter an evil word against your God. What happened? Their fiery faith gave God Jehovah respect in a heathen land.

Okay, where are we today? You might be in a heathen land, you might be in a heathenistic situation, but if you face the fiery challenges of this world with fireproof faith, men and women who don't even like you will respect you and the God that you serve. We need fireproof faith. Faith that won't give in and turn to ashes in the midst of a challenge. Faith that keeps us moving forward even when our enemies fire up the furnace of confusion, of challenge, of chaos, of disruption, of ugly-acting spirits. Face today with fireproof faith.

Faithful Prayer

[20] I went on praying and confessing my sin and the sin of my people, pleading with the Lord my God for Jerusalem, his holy mountain. [21] As I was praying, Gabriel, whom I had seen in the earlier vision, came swiftly to me at the time of the evening sacrifice. [22] He explained to me, "Daniel, I have come here to give you insight and understanding. [23] The moment you began praying, a command was given. And now I am here to tell you what it was, for you are very precious to God. Listen carefully so that you can understand the meaning of your vision.

Daniel 9:20-23

We have been studying different types of faith and each one is the act of trusting God. Faith needs to be sincere, it needs to be fireproof, it needs to be bold. You may ask me, where do I get that faith? It's not on the shelf, you can't buy it, you can't go to the library and check it out. Faith comes from the Lord. The very act of trusting in God will assure you that the Lord will give you whatever you need, whatever I need, whatever we need to do his will. Daniel was a person of prophecy and he wrote of what was going to happen to the nation of Israel and Judah. We can make that applicable to what is going on in our present time. Chapter 9, in Daniel, is full of numbers and it's full of symbolic images. We want to get the golden nugget out of this chapter. I encourage you to read, to study, to listen to some of your very good teachers and pastors and they will break down the number of weeks, the number of days, the week and a half, the 70 days. All of these have an actual meaning and application to our lives and it's fascinating and interesting.

But don't miss this. Daniel is praying. He's praying because he has done some research and the research reveals to him that God is true to his word. And what was said in the law, what Moses said, what the patriarchs of old said, and what was written in the ancient script was that, after a while, the Lord will get tired of fooling with them and with us. His hand of chastisement, which we defined in an earlier lesson as love, will come upon us. Now Daniel looked at that and said, this is going to be harsh. But, before he pleaded for leniency, he confessed. He said, Lord, I've done this, I could have done that better, and I didn't do the other. He also talked about his nation. His nation had wandered and walked away several times, almost as a lifestyle, from the loving arms of God. Notice in this prayer, the type of prayer that will result in faith that will push us into a life of obedience, that he was first honest about himself and about the nation. He confessed. He acknowledged the wonderful love of God, so he worshiped. Then he made his plea of leniency. Now, we get that backwards. As soon as we bow our heads, close our eyes, or get on our knees, or fold our hands, we tell the Lord what we want. But there was a season of confession, there was a season of adoration, and there was a season of petition. In other words, he praised the Lord, he confessed to the Lord and then he asked the Lord, could it be possible for this terrible chastisement to be moved from us.

An angel came. He acknowledged the fact that while Daniel was praying, he, Gabriel, came to encourage him and he told Daniel something that we're going to talk about in a few minutes. But I want you to pick up on this point. While Daniel was praying, the answer was on the way. That ought to encourage your heart. Sometimes you pray in the morning, you pray before you eat, you pray during the day, and you pray at night, sometimes some of us have learned to just go before the Lord in sincere and honest prayer and over a period of time. But notice this. Gabriel says, Daniel, when you started praying and when you asked for mercy, I was dispatched to bring you this news. The angel told him that things were going to get bad, and they're going to get better, then they're going to get bad again, but the end result, when the Lord gets through with you, when the Lord gets through with the nation of Israel and Judah, his will would have been done and we all will be better off for it.

We need to pray for our nation. I know we have a lot to discuss in terms of who did what and who said what. I understand that but we shouldn't dwell on that. Let's lift up our leaders in prayer. Let's pray for our senators, our Congress people, our mayors and our council people, our educational superintendents, and all of our elected officials. Let's pray for our president and let's pray for our president's family. Let's pray for those in the cabinet, let's pray for all of those elected officials. Let's ask the Lord to give them the wisdom to deal with this present time because, just like in Daniel's day, the news was bad, and it was getting worse.

Daniel went to the Lord. He didn't just hang out on the corner of CNN and NBC and CBS. He went to the Lord. He didn't build a box in the middle of the square in protest of this, that, and the other. Sometimes it's good to bring attention to a situation but before we protest, let's pray. Remember that the very act of prayer will dispatch ministering angels to me and to you and to the nation. The Lord is on his way. He is. He's on his way. He has promised that. One day, and one day very soon, we will see that angel and he or she will be announcing the presence of God almighty above all others. What we're dealing with now will be over. In the meantime, prayer can effect change in our present state of affairs. From our heart to the heart of our elected officials to our pastors and teachers, let's not forget to pray.

There's a correlation between faith and obedience. If you trust God, you will obey Him. If you don't trust God, you will not obey Him. You will not do what he says. Sometimes I go to the doctor and the doctor says, take this three times a day. I'll come back home and even though I have not been to medical school don't know anything about being a physician, I'll decide that

I'll take the pills twice a day or once a day or skip a day. I have paid dearly for my homemade way of dealing with my physical condition because I thought I knew more than the doctor and I thought the doctor needed my help. I didn't trust what she was telling me. If I had trusted the doctor, I would have saved myself and my family a lot of pain and grief and discomfort. I trust God, so I will do what he tells me. I trust God, so I will develop a sense of obedience that's reflected in my faith walk. Lord, I trust you. I may not understand, but I trust you. If you've asked me to do it, and he has, in his word, I'm going to endeavor to do it.

We've got a lot to pray for, right? Daniel is right on time. Let's pray and the end result of our prayer is going to be faith. The end result of our faith, trust in God, is going to be obedience to do his will.

Pastor Walter Henry Cross

For the Younger Scholars

Sweet Samples from Scripture

Santa Claus Is a Friend of Mine

Today, I want to tell you about a good friend of mine. He goes by many names: Kris Kringle, Father Christmas, Papa Noel. His name around here is Santa Claus, Saint Nick or Santa. In many parts of the world he has a different name. I'm going to tell you what's going on with Santa Claus.

First, let's look at the Bible in Luke 18:16.

> *16 But Jesus called them to him, saying, "Let the children come to me, and do not hinder them, for to such belongs the kingdom of God."*

It says that Jesus called the children unto himself and he said, let the little children come to me. Do not hinder or bother them. Do not restrict them, but let them come to me, for they are the kingdom of heaven. That's you. He's saying you are the kingdom of heaven. Jesus loved children.

Now, once upon a time there was a preacher, just like me, but in another part of the world. He loved children also. He had a lot of different names and we know him as St. Nicholas. Back then, his name was Father Nicholas, and he was concerned about the young children who did not have a mother or father.

Let me tell you what he did. He got some coal that you burn in the stove to stay warm; he got some wood and some kindling that you put to make a fire; and he put all that stuff in a bag with some money and put it across his back. That's where Santa gets his little bag from. During the night, Father Nicholas would go to orphanages or to where children were sleeping. He would take the money, gold coins, he would take the wood and

kindling, and he would take the coal for fuel and he would leave it on the doorstep or he would throw it through a window.

Now, this became a legend. A legend is a story about a person. Boys and girls, men and women, as you grow and as you develop, you will become a legend as well. Let me tell you about this legend. It grew and grew and grew; there were many similar stories because there were other preachers who felt a need to help little kids just like some of you sitting here. And they would take gifts; they would take wood and coal and food and clothing to the orphanages and in each different country where that happened, they had a different name for that priest.

> **Now, this became a legend. A legend is a story about a person. Boys and girls, men and women, as you grow and as you develop, you will become a legend as well.**

Now, let me tell you why Santa — no matter what you call him — carries a lantern. Father Christmas goes out at night, and he needs the lantern to light his way. He also has a little Christmas tree that he carries because he wants to help decorate the orphanage when he gets there. In his bag, he has money and supplies for the orphanage and he also has a big, heavy coat because a lot of times it would be wintertime when folks needed help. And that's the legend of St. Nicholas or Santa Claus.

Now, why does Santa Claus look the way he looks today? He looks a little different than St. Nicholas used to look. St. Nicholas, or Father Christmas, used to look very old-fashioned. But today's image of Santa Claus was the invention of the Coca-Cola Company. Years ago, the Coca-Cola Company had an artist paint a picture of Santa Claus. The artist painted him jolly and round. He was short and he had these red pants and coat with white fur trim. Actually, the first Santa Claus, or

Father Christmas, wore a robe that was heavy, and the color was green or sometimes purple. And that's how the legend of Santa Claus came to be.

So, guess who's coming to town on December the 25th, on Christmas Eve night? Santa Claus is coming to town. But I want to tell you about someone else who is coming: Jesus Christ, the Son of God, and he's coming for little girls and little boys like you. He's coming to bring you joy, not pain. He's coming to bring love, not hate. And he doesn't have to wait until December the 25th. Any time you open your heart and say, "Come Lord Jesus," he will come and be with you.

Sweet Samples from Scripture

Frosty The Snowman's Coming Back

Today I want to talk about someone who shows up every year about this time when the weather starts getting cold. Frosty the Snowman. He shows up on the lawns of many people as a Christmas decoration. He'll be in the parades and he'll be downtown. He's probably around your community. You'll see him flashing in the windows and all of his people will be with him, his little frosty children and his little frosty wife. Frosty is a cool dude, you know, he's about 32 degrees, so he's really cool. I like old Frosty.

Frosty is the person we're going to focus on today to tell you another story that's from the Bible. The story begins with a question. In Acts 1:11 an angel asks the apostles, Why are you still looking up? Because the same Jesus that you saw going up will come back the same way for his kingdom.

That scripture is talking about Jesus the Christ, who is the son of God, and who was mistreated by some very mean people. They hurt him and they hurt him so bad that he expired, he died, he passed away. They hurt him because he kept teaching and preaching the truth and he kept telling people how they could live in a way that would make the Father in Heaven happy. Well, some people didn't like that, so they got rid of him.

They thought he was gone for good but let me tell you what happened. Jesus got up from being murdered and walked around again in the same community, in the same place. He stayed a month and a week, about 40 days, almost six weeks, and in today's scripture we see him being lifted up like in an elevator; being lifted up by a cloud going back to his Father who

is in Heaven. But the people were so sad that he was gone that they couldn't move, they were just fixed there, and they kept looking up, looking up, hoping that he would come back. And that's when the angel said, this same Jesus that you saw going up is coming back again. And he is! He's coming to get me and you. That means we've got to get ready for Jesus to come back, because we want to go home with him and be with him forever.

Now, let's get back to Frosty. Whenever you see him, he's got that pipe in his mouth. We're working on Frosty. This is a no-no today. No smoking, okay. No one needs to be smoking, including Frosty. He's kind of young, but he's coming along, we're working on him. Frosty told the children one day, he was out playing and they're sliding down the hill and going ice skating, and all the stuff that children like to do in the snow. Frosty said, "The sun is hot." He began to melt in the sun. Frosty said, "I can't stay and play, but I will come back another day." Jesus said, "I'm going to leave and go to my Father, but I am coming back."

He's coming back, little ones, he's coming back on Christmas morning. But you don't have to wait for Christmas morning. He's coming back any day that you say yes to Jesus, "Come into my heart, come in today, come in to stay." Just like Frosty promised he's coming back, Jesus promised he's coming back, and we need to be ready. Every time you see Frosty in somebody's yard, on somebody's porch, in a coloring book, in a window downtown, wherever you see Frosty the Snowman or whenever you hear the song about Frosty the Snowman, think about Jesus coming back for me and for you.

Pastor Walter Henry Cross

Rudolph The Red-Nosed Reindeer Was Different

I want to reacquaint you with a dear friend of mine, Rudolph the red-nosed reindeer. Remember him? Rudolph was different. Rudolph was one of the reindeers-in-training to be used on Christmas Eve night, so the story goes, to take Santa around the world. I want to talk about Rudolph being different.

In the Old Testament, a man named David was the king of Israel. But I'm going to tell you how he got there. King David was preceded (meaning there was another king before him) by a king named Saul. Saul misbehaved. He didn't do everything the Lord told him to do. And when you don't do everything that your parents, your teachers, your guardians, your aunties and uncles, tell you to do, if you don't do the right thing the right way, there are consequences. Something may happen to you that may not be pleasant. I don't want you to be scared, but I do want you to be good.

So, Saul was going to be replaced. God told one of his preachers to go and find a new king. The Lord said, I'll tell you the direction, I'll tell you the right house, and when you get there you go in and you ask the owner of the house — in this case it was a man named Jesse — to look at his sons. Now, here's the criteria: don't look for height, don't look for *stature* (that means size), don't look at what they look like, just the one that I'm going to pick is the one that you're going to *anoint* (that means putting some oil on his head for a sign that he was approved of God). Then they have a big party, they have a big barbecue, they called it a sacrifice, they take an animal, put it on the grill and they cook it up real good and that was to celebrate the new king of Israel.

So, Samuel went to Jesse's house and had to go through all eight of Jesse's sons. David was number eight. Of course, being a proud papa, Jesse wanted all of his sons to make a good impression. Most of them were good-looking, tall, handsome, and had radiant hair. He probably wouldn't pick me. I'm like David, I'm different. Have you ever been different? Have you ever felt different? David was different. David was not in the house with the rest of them. He didn't stay around the ranch like the rest of them. He was way out in the field keeping the sheep. That was the lowest job on the ranch. He didn't work with the fine horses, the cattle; he didn't groom the animals. He was out there with the old smelly, dirty, nasty sheep and he had to stay way away from the ranch because the aroma, the smell of the sheep, would irritate the other animals, so he was isolated. That means he was out there by himself.

But God told Samuel, not these seven, I want the one that's different. Jesse said, "I have another boy but he's red headed, he's different. I have another boy and he's not at home, he's far away. His name is David, but he's short and dark-skinned; surely he couldn't be a king." And Samuel told Jesse, that's the one, that's the one the Lord wants and I'm going to sit here while you send someone out to get him.

David comes, not knowing what's going on, if he's in trouble, or if something has happened. His father said, This man of God wants to see you. Then Samuel goes through the ceremony and makes him king of Israel, even though he was different. David went from herding sheep to being the king.

Don't let being different stop you. It certainly didn't stop Rudolph. The song says that they made fun of Rudolph the red-nosed reindeer. Everywhere he would go, his nose would light up red. I can see him now. All the other reindeer wouldn't let him play in the reindeer games. If they had reindeer Olympics, he had to stay home. They would raise a little hoof, point at him, and say look at him over there with that red nose. Something's wrong with him. See, he's different, he doesn't

fit in, he's too different. Of course that made Rudolph feel left out. The word excluded comes to mind. He was excluded, not included, he was left out, he was not made a part of.

But what happened? Well, you know the story. It was foggy one Christmas Eve, and everybody heard Santa say, Rudolph, the different one, Rudolph, the odd one, Rudolph with your nose so bright, will you guide my sleigh tonight? He went from being back in the barn to being head of the sleigh.

He was still different. You may be different. Someone may have talked to you and told you that you were different. You may feel left out, but you may be the one leading the way through the fog of this world one day. David was different, but David became king. This Christmas season look for Rudolph. He'll be blinking out in front yards, he'll be on top of somebody's housetop just a-blinking. Look for him in Christmas displays everywhere you go. You may even have a Rudolph at your house. And every time you think about him, think that Rudolph was different, but he went from being back at the barn to being at the head of the sleigh. You don't have to be back of anybody. Be different, be great, be Christ-centered.

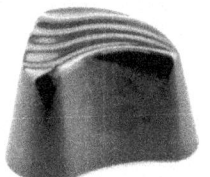

About the Author
Cross

Pastors Dr. Angela and Walter Cross

What an honor that my husband Walter Henry Lee Cross, known affectionaltely to me as Cross would ask me to write About the Author.

What can I say? Cross is a man on a mission, fulfilling every part. As son, as brother, as husband, as dad, as granddad, as uncle, as pastor, as mentor, as friend. Cross' love for Jesus the Christ compels his genuine love for people. What a people person, that's how we met and what a meeting. This beautiful man with beautiful brown eyes from Chattanooga, Tennessee who attended Howard High School, who never meets a stranger took his learning on the road when he entered Tennessee State University in Nashville, Tennessee. And it didn't stop there.

Cross is a connoisseur of so many things, people being one of them, I tell you that's how we met. Cross saw me standing there in a bookstore and said hello. That's how it all got started and I believe God orchestrated the rest. Thanks be to God for knowing what we need even when we may not know. Cross likes learning not only about people but about God, so this desire for God took him on an expedition through the halls of learning and Candler School of Theology at Emory University in Atlanta, Georgia.

And Cross has not stopped learning. Cross has a fascinating mind, that you will love as you digest these sweet words of life. Cross finds a lesson in everything and I do mean everything. You will find this read refershing, tasty, sustainable, and full of Godly wisdom. So sit down in a cozy place and taste and see that the Lord is Good!

May you know God is blessing you every day.

Faith, Hope, Love,

Rev. Doctor Angela Hardy Cross

Taste and See

If you'd like to be the first to know about new publications from Pastor Walter Cross, and the upcoming audio editions of *Sweet Samples from Scripture*, check out PastorWalterCross.com. There, while supplies last, you can also download a free coupon for a sweet sampler set of four chocolates from Bradley's Gift and Home on N. Peter's Road in Knoxville. Visit Bradley's online at shopbradleys.com